birthdays are
good for you-
the more
you have,
the longer
you live!

June 9 2009

Hope you enjoy this day & all
the days to come...

Deb & Carrie DeFosset

LOVE
ADDS
a LITTLE
CHOCOLATE

LOVE ADDS a LITTLE CHOCOLATE

*100 Stories to
Brighten Your Day
and Sweeten Your Life*

MEDARD LAZ

CHARIS

SERVANT PUBLICATIONS

ANN ARBOR, MICHIGAN

Charis Books is an imprint of Servant Publications.

The author and publisher express their appreciation to those whose stories and excerpts were selected for this book. Every effort has been made to trace all copyright owners; if any acknowledgment has been inadvertently omitted, the publisher will gladly make the necessary correction in the next printing. Acknowledgments appear on pages 211-217.

Published by Servant Publications
P.O. Box 8617
Ann Arbor, Michigan 48107

Cover design: Paul Higdon
Author photo: Kramer Photo, Palatine, Illinois. Used by permission.

97 98 99 00 01 10 9 8 7 6 5 4 3 2 1

Printed in the United States of America
ISBN 1-56955-027-1

LIBRARY OF CONGRESS CATALOGING-IN-PUBLICATION DATA

Love adds a little chocolate : stories to brighten your day and sweeten your life / [compiled by] Medard Laz.
    p.   cm.
ISBN 1-56955-027-1
1. Christian life—Anecdotes.   I. Laz, Medard.
BV4517.L68   1997
242—dc21   96-52893
                                                                    CIP

CONTENTS

2
Love Adds a Little Chocolate...
TO CARING

3
Love Adds a Little Chocolate...
TO UNDERSTANDING

6
Love Adds a Little Chocolate...
TO ACHIEVING

7
Love Adds a Little Chocolate...
TO WISDOM

<u>8</u>
Love Adds a Little Chocolate...
TO CHRISTMAS

THANKS

Love added *a lot* of chocolate to the pages of this book as it moved from conception to completion...

To the many women, men, and children whose identities are obscured on each of the following pages, but whose courage, heroism, goodness, and love bring hope and joy to all of us;

To all of those authors who allowed me the privilege of including their treasured stories and to Margaret France and Richard J. Reece for their kind assistance in locating several authors;

To all the permissions editors who graciously accepted my numerous calls and got back to me with the necessary copyright permissions;

To Heidi Hess, my managing editor, for her superb editing, her unwavering support, and her attention to frustrating details;

To Bert Ghezzi, my editor and friend, who had faith in me and in the project since the beginning and who helped remove every obstacle along the way;

To the entire staff at Servant Publications who gave of their hearts to see this book completed, especially Jeanne Mullins, Lonni Collins Pratt, Diane Bareis, and Paul Rzepka;

To Paul Higdon and the design staff who created the look and the feel of the book;

To Joseph Girzone for his encouragement and ongoing support for my work;

To Laurel Burns, whose insightful comments and support were most helpful;

And to Sandy and Rich Chlebos who stepped in to help when I needed their assistance at the last minute.

My deepest gratitude.

*That it will never come again
is what makes life so sweet.*
EMILY DICKINSON

INTRODUCTION

SO MANY PEOPLE SEEM TO BE SEARCHING for a life that has meaning. The simple truth is that every person already possesses a life that has a tremendous worth and value. Behind every face is a beating heart, a questing spirit, and a personal story. We want more than anything to be able to get in touch with the experience of what it means to be fully human and fully alive.

This collection of inspirational stories speaks to this need. These stories tap into a common ground of adventures that leads each of us into the quiet depths of our souls. Our experience of mystery, our quest for identity (Who am I, really?), the haunting reality of our mortality, our search for love and a sense of belonging—these are universal to us all. They echo a voice deep within us that longs to be heard.

All of the stories related here are fundamental human experiences that herald a patterned response in our imaginations. Why? Because we all draw from a common spiritual source that provides us with hope and encouragement as we journey through a labyrinth of life's adventures. You will discover that many of the stories here are truly *your stories,* revealing an immediate and compelling truth about your life.

Each story trusts you to make your own interpretation. There is no moralizing or preaching to be found here. Yet each story arises from our own collective human unconscious—inviting us to risk, to trust, to hope, to love, to surrender, and finally... *to add a little chocolate! Enjoy!*

Medard Laz

O N E

LOVE ADDS *a* LITTLE CHOCOLATE... TO LIFE

---

*Love begins
when a person feels
another person's need
to be as important
as his own.*
HARRY STACK SULLIVAN

PEANUTS reprinted by permission of United Features Syndicate, Inc.

Love Adds a Little Chocolate

A house is a house—until love comes through the door, that is. And love intuitively goes around sprinkling that special brand of angel dust that transforms a house into a very special home for very special people: your family.

Money, of course, can build a charming house, but only love can furnish it with a feeling of home.

Duty can pack an adequate sack lunch, but love may decide to enclose a little love note inside.

Money can provide a television set, but love controls it and cares enough to say no and take the guff that comes with it.

Obligation sends the children to bed on time, but love tucks the covers in around their necks and passes out kisses and hugs (even to teenagers!).

Obligation can cook a meal, but love embellishes the table with a potted ivy trailing around slender candles.

Duty writes many letters, but love adds a joke or a picture or a fresh stick of gum inside.

Compulsion keeps a sparkling house. But love and prayer stand a better chance of producing a happy family.

Duty gets offended quickly if it isn't appreciated, but love learns to laugh a lot and to work for the sheer joy of doing it.

Obligation can pour a glass of milk, but quite often, love adds a little chocolate.

Author Unknown

Encounter in a Boutique

She was a bag lady. At least she looked like one. And she seemed to sing her conversation, repeating each statement or question about three times.

She entered the boutique and my life shortly after noon. It wasn't a particularly cold day, but then, it wasn't shelter she was seeking. Rather, she sang out her desire and she sang it thrice: "A pair of ski pants. A pair of ski pants. A pair of ski pants." This got everybody's attention. Some noses went up a level. Some backs turned. One set of eyes couldn't resist peering over a shoulder to sneak a look.

Why me? I moaned inwardly. I was just a part-time book-keeper. I had never worked the floor with this higher-classed clientele whose charge cards I tallied and billed from the room upstairs. I simply had been pressed into sales-clerkdom by a small sales staff who wished to take the owner to lunch in honor of her birthday. Sure, I'd handle the store. I could do it for an hour.

But now this. A larger part of me than I like to admit resented the unlikely customer. We never got bag ladies in *this* shop. Yet, my snobbishness surprised me, and so I softened a bit under self-reproach. In retrospect, I can't really recall how she was dressed. I don't even remember if she actually carried a bag, this bag lady. It doesn't matter. She was out of her place. Except she didn't seem to know it. She beamed with graciousness, and innocence... as unselfconscious as a newborn.

I looked down at my own light tan cords, neat but hardly new, and I was reminded with a resentful twinge that I was a bit out of station myself. It didn't help my suffering self-confidence to realize that I was probably closer to this bag lady than the clique of customers I knew were lying in subtle wait to pass judgment on how I handled such an intruder. Oh, they were unobtrusive, all right, studiedly so. And I felt vulnerable to the exposure of my blueless blood. I would have to quickly dispatch this unwanted creature with aplomb, and, of course, politeness.

But as I approached this objectification of my own internal demons, she smiled so warmly that my hardline offense melted. I responded in kind. "Can I help you?"

"These would be fine. These would be fine. These would be fine," she sang in a high-pitched lilt. She was lifting a pair of famous-maker ski pants from an antique display bin. They were marked 50 percent off. They also were marked size 18, much too large for this small-framed woman.

"I'm sorry," I answered. "Those pants are all size 18. Too large, I'm afraid. Could I show you some others?"

The smile never left her. "Thank you, thank you, thank you," she sing-songed. "You're a lovely lady. You're a lovely lady. You're a lovely lady."

Now why did she have to say that? Couldn't she see the embarrassment I felt for her?

Yet, I felt flattered by this incorrigible bag lady's praise... and my neediness disgusted me. Then, something else happened.

I was suddenly relieved I had not given in to my baser instincts to dismiss this "lesser" sister of mine. I felt shame flush through me for having considered using her to the approval of my su-peer-iors.

I thanked her for coming in, this street creature, and I wished her a good day. She smiled widely. Was there really a space where a tooth should have been?

But that smile... Perkily touching her right forefinger to her cheek, she challenged me, singing:

"A kiss on the cheek and I'll be gone. A kiss on the cheek and I'll be gone. A kiss on the cheek and I'll be gone." I could almost hear the clientele gasping.

The moment expanded and stopped. I had seemingly unlimited time to assess my feelings and motives. I could express disdain. I could acquiesce out of pity. Or I could simply comply.

Oh hell, I kissed her on the cheek. Time began again. The lady with the bag looked at me one final time. Was the smile gone? (Strange, I can't remember her face.) But I do remember what she said as she turned to leave the shop.

"I am an angel of the Lord," the woman told me, "and you shall be blessed the rest of your days."

Gloria J. Gibson

It's better to have a rich soul than to be rich.
OLGA KORBUT

Bootless Tears

As a fledgling teacher I had over fifty students in my second-grade class. Snowy days were, at best, horrendous, with requests from every child for help with outer clothing and boots. One afternoon at dismissal time, all the boots had been claimed except one pair which had been pushed into a corner. In the middle of the group of students stood a little girl, crying. "I can't find my boots!" she wailed.

Pointing to the pair in the corner, I said, "There are your boots."

She insisted they were not hers.

"How do you know they're not yours?" I asked.

Her blue eyes engaged mine solemnly, as she declared, "Mine had snow on them."

Sr. Mary Corita Sweeney, R.S.M.

Grown-ups never understand anything for themselves,
and it is tiresome for children to be always and forever
explaining things to them.
ANTOINE DE SAINT-EXUPÉRY

All the Time in the World

Whidle at the park one day, a woman sat down next to a man on a bench near a playground. "That's my son over there," she said, pointing to a little boy in a red sweater who was gliding down the slide.

"He's a fine looking boy," the man said. "That's my son on the swing in the blue sweater." Then, looking at his watch, he called to his son. "What do you say we go, Todd?"

Todd pleaded, "Just five more minutes, Dad. Please? Just five more minutes." The man nodded and Todd continued to swing to his heart's content.

Minutes passed and the father stood and called again to his son. "Time to go now?" Again Todd pleaded, "Five more minutes, Dad. Just five more minutes." The man smiled and said, "OK."

"My, you certainly are a patient father," the woman responded.

The man smiled and then said, "My older son Tommy was killed by a drunk driver last year while he was riding his bike near here. I never spent much time with Tommy and now I'd give anything for just five more minutes with him. I've vowed not to make the same mistake with Todd. He thinks *he* has five more minutes to swing. The truth is, I get five more minutes to watch him play."

Author Unknown

Sacrifice

A father tried to teach his seven-year-old daughter the meaning of sacrifice. He explained that the finest gift a person can give is some cherished possession, one that the person values very much.

On his birthday the father found pinned to his coat a large sheet of paper on which his daughter had laboriously printed with red crayon: "You are my faverit Daddy and I luv you heeps. My present to you is what I likes best. It is in your poket."

In his pocket he found a strawberry lollipop that he had given her a week before. It hadn't been licked once.

Author Unknown

To teach is to learn twice.
JOSEPH JOUBERT

New Life for an Old Skirt

Our family's first house was near the quarry, near a poorer section of town. These people were so poor that one family of eight lived in a chicken coop just up the road from us. Almost all kids then wore a lot of hand-me-downs; we thought nothing of it. One of my mother's piano students who was older than us, for instance, would pass on something she'd outgrown; our mother, who made beautiful clothes, would pass on our outgrown things to other friends. And we had clothing drives at our elementary school all the time because these children from the quarry had no one to hand-me-down to or from.

I had a favorite skirt my Mom had made—a black border print with clowns all around it. As I grew, she kept letting out the hem until it had gone as far as it would go. Then she put it in a clothing drive.

Shortly after I saw my skirt on practically the only kid in the school smaller and skinnier than I was. I came home saying, "Mom, Lois has my skirt on."

She said, "Now don't say anything about that skirt. Don't tell her it was yours. You enjoyed it. You're too tall. She'll enjoy it." She made me think about Lois's feelings, something I've not forgotten since.

Amy Holloway

Surprise!

There was a twelve-year-old girl named Monica who hated sharing a bedroom with her six-year-old sister. She longed for the day when she would have a room all to herself. It seems that her father had much the same idea to have a room to himself.

Monica's dad was attending night school and he looked forward to the day when he would have a room where he could study in a quiet place that was away from his noisy family. Throughout the hot summer months he drew up his plans for the new room. Once the foundation was poured, he put up the walls, did the plastering, and installed the wiring and the windows. The work proceeded slowly, but finally the walls were painted and the carpet was installed.

One day when Monica came home from school, she discovered that the bedroom she shared with her sister had been completely rearranged. She became very angry with her sister for having torn apart the room. She ran down the hallway into the new addition to the house to lodge a complaint with her parents.

Her parents were standing there ready to greet her with a shout of "Surprise!" To Monica's astonishment, she discovered that all her possessions had been moved to the new addition.

"Daddy came to realize, dear, you needed your own room," her mother said. "So he came up with the idea that you should have this as your room."

Author Unknown

A Warm Hand on a Cold Day

It wasn't precisely what the young hitchhiker wanted, but it was better than nothing. The unidentified hitchhiker's thumb stuck hopefully in the air asking for a ride. As the day wore on his hand was growing red from the cold.

A shiny, red Corvette crept past the youth in the slow-moving traffic. As it passed the hitchhiker, the window on the passenger's side of the car was rolled down and a pair of gloves flew out to the thumber.

The young man put the gloves on, waved a thank you to the motorist, and continued his thumbing in the snowy 28-degree weather, but now with a pair of warm hands.

Author Unknown

The best place to find a helping hand is at the end of your arm.
ELMER LETERMAN

The Friendly Fisherman

~ ♥ ~

About six people were fishing offshore when we arrived. My husband picked up his fishing rod, bait, and tackle box, and headed down the river. A young man was standing in my favorite spot, so I moved about five yards from him near a big tree at the water's edge.

With my first cast, my bobber flew off. As I reeled in my line, the young man asked if I had another bobber. "I'll have to find my husband," I said.

He laid down his pole, opened his tackle box, and fitted a nice red bobber on my line. "Bait up," he said with a friendly grin. In a few minutes he pulled in a good-sized bass.

Meanwhile, I had managed to get my line all tangled up. "Having trouble?" he asked. When I nodded, he began working on my line and finally got everything in order. "Bait up," he said, encouragingly. Then he pulled in another bass.

"I have a bite," I yelled, minutes later. I tried to reel in the fish but nothing happened. "You've snagged a log," he said. Then he tried to free my hook. After walking up and down he succeeded. The other people fishing nearby were beginning to enjoy the entertainment.

My next cast sent the bobber, sinker, and fishhook up in the tree. The friendly young man laid down his pole and helped me get the line out of the tree. We fished in silence for a little while. Then I cast again, and somehow the line wound around me and the hook stuck into the back of my pants. "Having trouble?" he asked. He worked and worked, and finally got the hook out.

When he was ready to leave, he pulled up his stringer of

fish and said, "Here, take these fish." As he walked toward his car, I said, "I'm sorry I spoiled your day." He turned around and started laughing. "Lady, you *made* it."

Katherine Karras

The love we give away is the only love we keep.
ELBERT HUBBARD

Good News

I remember one night being called to the hospital to visit someone who was very sick and in intensive care. It was after midnight and I had to enter the hospital through the Emergency entrance. Most of the hall lights in the hospital had been dimmed so the patients could get to sleep. Everything was quiet and still as I headed down the hallway looking for a room number.

Suddenly a woman darted out from behind the curtains in one of the patient rooms and ran out into the hallway. This total stranger came up to me and pulled on the lapels of my overcoat. Her face was beaming with joy. "He's going to make it! He's so much better! The doctor says he's going to make it!" With that the woman headed down the long hallway to where the telephones were located.

I had never seen the woman before, nor did I know whom she was talking about. Possibly it was her husband, her son, or her father. I presumed it was someone very close and dear to her. Obviously she had just gotten the good news and she needed to share it with the first person she met. It made no difference if she knew me or not.

It was good news, and good news like that just has to be shared.

Medard Laz

Shared joy is double joy;
and shared sorrow is half-sorrow.
<small>SWEDISH PROVERB</small>

Outward Appearances

A man and a woman who had been corresponding with each other across the country via the Internet eventually fell in love. They were dying to meet each other in person. They agreed to fly into Chicago and meet at the airport. Since they had never seen each other, they came up with a plan that would help them recognize each other. The woman would wear a green scarf and a green hat and have a green carnation pinned to her coat. Since her flight was due to arrive shortly before his, she would be at the gate waiting for his arrival.

When the man disembarked from his plane, he immediately began searching for her. In a matter of moments he spied a woman standing off from the crowd with a green scarf, a green hat, and a green carnation pinned to her coat. His heart sank. She was one of the plainest women he had ever seen. He was almost ready to get back on the plane without even going up to her. He felt an obligation so he walked over to the woman, tapped her on the shoulder, smiled, and then introduced himself.

Without hesitation the woman blurted out, "What is this all about? Is this some kind of a TV show or what? I have no idea who you are. That woman over there behind that pillar gave me twenty dollars to wear all these things. She said it was important." When the man looked over at the woman standing by the pillar, he caught sight of one of the most beautiful women he had ever seen.

The man approached the woman and they made their formal introductions. Later in the conversation she explained her ruse. "All my life men have wanted to be with me, to be my friend, all because of my outward appearance. They consider me beautiful. This is why I started a relationship over the Internet. I wanted to meet someone who would love me, not just for my outward appearance, but for what I am inside."

Author Unknown

The greatest happiness in life is the conviction that we are loved, loved for ourselves, or rather, loved in spite of ourselves.
VICTOR HUGO

When God Says "No"

A tall, attractive woman in her early thirties stopped me after church one Sunday morning and asked if she could see me for a few minutes. I had never seen her before, but I obliged and ushered her into my office. When we were seated, she told me that she had been to one of my services three years before. Then she recounted for me a true story I had used to introduce my message that day.

*   *   *

There was once a little girl who wanted a Barbie doll for her very own. Every evening the little girl would kneel down to say her prayers, and remind God of her wish. "Please God, give me a Barbie for Christmas."

Christmas came and went, but there was no doll for this little girl.

The girl's birthday was at the end of January, and so she once again added a special petition each night for a new Barbie doll. "Please, God, I don't want anything else. Just my Barbie." But when she opened her birthday presents, there was no doll to be found.

Valentine's Day was next, and the girl redoubled her efforts. "I don't want any candy, God. Just a Barbie, please." Her brother, who had been listening to her nighttime prayers all along, grew tired of hearing about the doll. "Why don't you just give up?" he asked her impatiently. "God isn't answering your prayers."

"But God *is* answering my prayers," insisted the little girl.

"How could God be answering your prayers?" replied her brother. "Christmas has come and gone, and you just had your birthday. And you still don't have your doll. God is not answering your prayers."

"Yes, he is," she repeated. "God is telling me NO!"

*   *   *

The woman in my office finished telling me the story. Then she said to me, "You know, when I first heard you tell that story I was very upset by it. There was a guy in my life at that time, and I wanted things to work out between us in the worst way. I prayed and prayed that God would help me to win his heart. But it didn't work out the way I'd hoped...." Her voice broke and trailed off. Rising from her seat, she went to the door, then turned back to face me, her eyes full of tears. "I just wanted to thank you for that story. When that little girl said, 'God is telling me NO!' I knew I had my answer, too. It just took me a while to accept it."

Medard Laz

Every human being on earth is born with a tragedy, and it isn't original sin. He's born with the tragedy that he has to grow up. A lot of people don't have the courage to do it.
HELEN HAYES

Loving You

The next time I have the urge to speak negatively
or rudely to you, I'll swallow and be silent.
Loving you doesn't give me license for rudeness.

If I can't be generous and supportive, I'll at least
try not to stand in your way.
Loving you means wanting you to grow.

I won't put my problems onto you. You have
enough problems, I'm certain, and you don't need mine.
My love should simplify your life, not complicate it.

I don't always have to be right. I can accept
the fact that you are right as often as I am.
Loving is sharing with each other.
If I already know I'm right, all the time,
I'll never profit from your insight.

I don't always have to be running the show.
Loving is an ebb and flow.
Sometimes I'll need to give in.
And at other times I'll need to take control.

I don't have to be perfect, nor do you.
Love is a celebration of our humanness, not our perfection.

I can give up wanting to change you. If I want
you in my life, the best thing for both of us is for me
to accept you as you are.
After all, love is moving forward together in mutual growth.

I don't need to place blame. Since I'm an adult
who makes decisions based upon personal experience,
there is no one to blame for a poor decision except myself.
Love puts the responsibility where it belongs.

I can give up expectations. To wish is one thing,
to expect is another. One brings hope, the other can
bring pain. Love is free of expectations.

Leo Buscaglia

---

*The entire sum of existence is the magic of
being needed by just one person.*
V. PUTNAM

The Missing Piece

A husband and wife were celebrating fifty years of married life together—their golden wedding anniversary. They had a blow-out celebration at a hall with their children, grandchildren, and their many relatives and friends. When they finally made their way home from the big party that was thrown for them, they were tired and happy to be home again to peace and quiet.

They were so busy with everyone that day and so excited with the grand event that neither of them had eaten much during the day or evening. So they decided, before going to bed, to have a little snack of coffee with homemade bread and butter. They were sitting at the kitchen table. The husband took out a new loaf of bread and handed the end piece (the heel) to his wife of fifty years. She immediately went into a rage.

She shouted at him, "For fifty years you have been dumping the heel of the bread on me. I just won't take it from you anymore. You could care less about what I like." On and on her anger raged, all ignited by his offering her the heel of the bread. He sat there in absolute astonishment over what he was hearing.

When she finally finished, he said to her quietly, "But, honey, it's my favorite piece."

Author Unknown

All the Unseen

Take a minute now:
count to yourself
all the people you'll talk to today —
teachers, friends, parents,
brothers, sisters.
Have you ever gone twenty-four hours
without talking to someone?
Each person on earth (billions of them)
is as much a marvel as you;
yet each person needs others.
We work together:
I don't have to reinvent arithmetic
to count my socks,
or plant wheat seeds
in order to eat bread next September.
Someone else has already done those things.
Is there a radio near your bed?
Turn it on and another amazing creature will
tell you the weather.
He got it from another
wonderful creature
who got it from instruments
made by another
and invented by yet another wonderful creature
who isn't even alive anymore.
How well off would you be
if this cold morning
you had to do everything alone:

make your own food,
house,
socks,
car?
Where would you be without all those unseen
people?
Isn't it incredible
how we share?
One more minute
before you get out of bed.
Think about one more thing.
Giraffes move gracefully;
bees share the invention of honey;
an antelope leaps quicker than you can think.

But no other animal
so far as I know
ever lies awake
in the gray morning,
eyes wide open,
amazed, thinking
how wonderful it is to wake up
as me.

Tim Stafford

Our Home

A reporter rushed to a fire where a house was steadily burning down to the ground. The entire structure was ablaze. The newsman noticed that there was a little boy standing nearby with his mom and dad watching everything go up in flames.

With sympathy in his voice the reporter said, "Son, it looks like you don't have a home any more."

The little boy looked up and responded courageously, "*We have a home*—we just don't have a house to put it in."

Author Unknown

Fear is that little darkroom where negatives are developed.
Michael Pritchard

Reruns

Stanley was a simple man, a man who lived an uncomplicated life—uncomplicated, that is, except for Miriam, his wife.

He worked hard at his eight-to-four job at the mill. When he was finished with work, he looked forward to a couple of beers with the guys, a good hot meal with the wife, and then his one pleasure: "Charlie's Angels" reruns.

This last thing he had to fight hard for. Usually right after supper Miriam had all kinds of work lined up for Stanley to do: mow the lawn, paint the porch, clean out the garage, fix the banister, dig the garden, repair the leaking faucet... on and on the list went, seemingly without end. All Stanley wanted to do was kick off his shoes, pop the top of a brew, and watch as three beautiful women brought justice to society.

"Stanley," Miriam's voice rasped like a hacksaw blade trying to cut through quarter-inch plate steel. "Stanley, are you down there? When are you going to take the storm windows down? I swear, it will be the middle of August and we won't have a single screen up. Stanley, are you listening to me?"

"Aw, Miriam, can't I have just a little quiet? Let me watch the Angels. I'll work on the windows when it's over."

"That's what you say every night. And what do you do? You fall asleep in your chair and nothing gets done."

"It'll get done, Miriam. I promise. Just let me watch my program."

Miriam's displeasure could be measured by the volume of the noise she made as she banged the pots and pans around while washing the dishes. She also muttered to herself, just loud enough to be heard but not understood.

He tuned in "Charlie's Angels" and tuned out Miriam. "Ah, it doesn't get much better than this."

But little did Stanley or Miriam know that this evening was not going to be like any of the others.

Stanley took a drink from his can of beer, looking down the length of the can in almost the same way as one would sight a gun, and listened as Charlie spoke with the Angels and Boswell, outlining their assignment. Suddenly the picture disappeared and the screen went dark.

"Miriam, is the power off?"

"Of course not! What are you talking about?"

"The set isn't working. Right in the middle of the program everything went blank."

Stanley knew what was coming even before Miriam said it. "Aw, that's a shame. Does that mean you will be able to do the windows now?"

"Miriam, will you please get off my back? I work hard at the mill. Is it too much to ask to come home to some peace and quiet? Honestly, it just isn't fair that..."

Stanley never finished his sentence for just then the television came to life again, only the program wasn't the same.

"What is this?" Stanley asked as he reached for the remote control and started to switch channels. "That's strange, all the channels are the same."

It was strange. Regular programming on every station had stopped. Now every channel showed another program that closely resembled a news broadcast but wasn't quite the same. "Miriam, come on down here and look at this."

Miriam sensed the effect on Stanley by the tone of his voice.

She descended the stairs to their family room, drying her hands on a hand-towel as she walked. "What's wrong?"

Stanley didn't look up. He could not divert his eyes from the changing images on the screen.

"What are you watching? What is it? Stanley, say something."

And then both of them sat silent—not another word was spoken. Stanley and Miriam just sat and watched.

The segments were brief, but there was no missing the message. Scene followed scene.... Scenes of Christians fighting Moslems in Beirut, Jews fighting Arabs in Palestine, Protestants fighting Catholics in Ireland, Contras fighting Sandanistas, emaciated Ethiopians, freezing homeless, abused children, glazed-eyed drug addicts, greedy pushers, prostitutes and willing "Johns," porno shops and crack houses, forgotten elderly, exiled AIDS victims, the poor, the exiled, criminals on death row... scene after scene of human injustice, deprivation, greed, and moral poverty. Stanley wiped a tear from his cheek with the back of his hand, and Miriam sniffed as she searched the pocket of her apron for her handkerchief.

Then the images changed to children laughing and playing, lovers walking hand in hand, nursing homes with parking lots filled with cars of visitors, neighbors giving neighbors a hand, the birth of a child, a successful bypass surgery.

Then, once again, the screen darkened. A voice, commanding but gentle, spoke: "You have just seen a small portion of what I see day after day. My vision has been granted to you so that you will know the truth, and the truth will set you free. This is my commandment: I am the Lord your God, you shall have no other gods. This is my commandment: Be fruitful, multiply, subdue the earth, and fill it. This is my commandment: Love one another as I have loved you."

Stanley and Miriam sighed deeply as though taking their first life-breath. They looked at one another in wonder. A change had come over them, but it was difficult to know what it was. They just sat and stared at the blank screen. Did they really see what they thought they had seen? Was it real? Was it a dream? Was it a hoax?

"Please stay tuned," the voice came from the speaker in the set. "We are experiencing technical difficulties and have temporarily lost control of our programming. We will resume our regular schedule as soon as—"

Once again the screen sprang to life. Boswell and the Angels looked knowingly at one another as they did every night when they had completed a successful mission. "Well Charlie," Boswell said into the conference phone speaker on his desk, "that wraps it up."

Stanley pressed the power button on his remote control. A

faint click signaled that the power had been turned off. He picked up his half-filled can of warm beer.

Miriam looked up. "Stanley, where are you going?"

"It's time to put the screens in the window. The fresh air will feel good."

James L. Henderschedt

Life is now in session.
Are you present?
B. COPELAND

Your Life Will Be Richer—If

Your life will be richer if on this day
You will make an effort to:
Mend a quarrel.
Search for a forgotten friend.
Dismiss a suspicion and replace it with trust.
Write a letter to someone who misses you.
Encourage someone who has lost faith.
Keep a promise.
Forget an old grudge.
Examine your demands on others, and vow to reduce them.
Fight for a principle.
Express your gratitude.
Overcome an old fear.
Take two minutes to appreciate the beauty of nature.
Tell someone you love them.
Tell them again.
And again.
And again.

Author Unknown

-----

*The aim of life is to spend it for
something that will outlast it.*
WILLIAM JAMES

LOVE ADDS *a* LITTLE CHOCOLATE... TO CARING

---

*The world will not care
what we know
until they know
that we care.*
GENE BARRON

PEANUTS reprinted by permission of United Features Syndicate, Inc.

She Always Played Peggy Sue

"Starting next Monday, this restaurant will become a non-smoking zone," read the sign on the door of my favorite diner. It's a small place that serves breakfast and lunch. The pancakes are light and fluffy, and the maple syrup is hot. And to tell you the truth, when the smoking-ban sign appeared, I was delighted.

I was raised in a family of non-smokers and non-drinkers. Not to mention the warnings that have surfaced in recent years about the dangers of smoking—all of this has only increased my distaste for the scent of cigarettes and cigars.

Still, in spite of myself, I felt a little sad for the blonde woman. For well over a year now, I'd noticed her every time I came to the diner for breakfast. She was buggy-whip thin. Her skin seemed transparent, and her hair seemed to be forever growing dark roots. It was lifeless hair, straight and limp. She looked, to my eyes, awfully ill.

I never saw her eat a thing. She would return to the counter again and again for more coffee. And she smoked. There never seemed to be a moment when the blonde woman wasn't puffing on a cigarette. She sat some distance from me, in the smoking section. Still, I always noticed her. And I pitied her. She seemed so alone, so sad, so sickly.

Now this little eating place, on top of good pancakes, also has an old-fashioned jukebox. Inside are recordings from the '50s and early '60s: the golden oldies of rock 'n' roll.

The blonde woman, cigarette in hand, would stand by that jukebox pouring coin after coin into it. Always, she played the same song, a recording called *Peggy Sue*, sung by the late Buddy Holly.

I cannot recall her ever playing any other tune. While she listened, the blonde woman would close her eyes. I'd find myself wondering if she was thinking about certain people or events from a long-ago era, the time the recording first was popular.

And so, when I saw the sign, I thought immediately of the blonde woman. I knew she likely would be forced to change her morning routine. Would she still come, giving up the cigarettes for coffee and Buddy Holly alone? I didn't think so.

But there's another person in this little tale. A young man with hair the color of fire and a face covered with freckles. He wasn't there every time I ate breakfast at the diner, but I saw him quite often. Judging by the business suit and brief-case, he was a young professional. He spoke to everybody, even those he didn't actually know. His "Good morning" was always warm and brisk.

Naturally, we offered salutations in return. Well, most of us. Not the blonde woman. She completely ignored the young man.

Indeed, she ignored just about everyone else, too. One day, I happened to be sitting close to the jukebox when the blonde woman put her money in. As Buddy Holly started to sing, I said, "I like that song." She just glared at me.

And so the day arrived. Smoking would not be allowed come morning. The blonde woman arrived as usual. No one would have guessed anything was about to change.

After a short time, the young man with the red hair arrived as well. To my surprise, he walked over to the table where the blonde woman was seated, drinking her coffee and smoking her cigarette.

He laid down a small bag. After a while, the woman opened the bag and took something out. She studied it for a few moments. Then she started to cry. She stood up and waved her gift. It looked like a cassette tape.

"It's got Buddy Holly singing *Peggy Sue* on it," she said.

The blonde woman left the diner soon after receiving her present. As she departed, she held the bag close. And when she passed the young man, she bent down and kissed his cheek.

On our way out, we stopped at the young man's table.

He knew why, and volunteered an explanation. "Two years ago," the young man told me and my friend, "my mother died from lung cancer. We tried so hard to convince her to stop smoking... my dad, my two sisters, and me. We prayed for her.

"One day, our parish priest told me that he believed my mom wasn't ever going to stop smoking. He said we should try to show her compassion. What she needed, the priest said, was to know her family still loved her.

"But I was angry," the young man explained, "so angry. I thought that if she really loved us, she would stop."

The young man paused to wipe a tear.

"This time, I didn't make the same mistake," he said. "This time, I wanted to show compassion while there was still time to do it."

Mary Louise Kitsen

The Good Samaritan

One day while I was extremely busy attending to our six children, the telephone rang just as I was ready to go out the door to take the girls to Brownies. It was a friend from church who was upset because her husband had left her.

My life was in constant turmoil, and I did not want to set one more moment aside for another unsolicited interruption, so I said, "I don't have time to talk, because I'm just ready to leave to run an errand."

I hadn't driven more than a mile before I was forced to come to a standstill due to a road construction project. I waited for over thirty minutes, and my having to sit at an idle for so long caused the car to overheat, and, sure enough, it stalled. I got out of the car, started waving my arms in the air to every passing motorist along the highway, but no one would stop.

Finally, forty minutes later, an elderly man pulled over, assessed the situation, and drove to the nearest filling station for some water. He came back and worked with my radiator until he got the car started again. After the man finished and was ready to leave, I said, "Thank you. I hope I haven't made you late for an important engagement."

He answered, "No problem, I was just on my way to the hospital to visit my wife, who had major surgery on her back yesterday. Besides, I couldn't just drive by without helping." He bid me a good day and left.

He was certainly a Good Samaritan. I told the children what a kind man he was for helping us and started down the highway again. Of course, we didn't make it to the Brownie meeting, so I got off at the next exit and headed home.

After supper I decided to visit my troubled friend. We spent over three hours together, and I didn't feel rushed at all. I learned from that experience that the more love I give to others, the more room I make for God's love.

Carol Goll Burris

No one knows his true character until he has run out of gas, purchased something on the installment plan, and raised an adolescent.
MARCELENE COX

Spilt Milk

At a busy intersection in New York City, a thirty-gallon can fell from a passing truck, spilling milk all over the intersection. The policeman halted traffic while the driver retrieved the can.

The policeman was about to blow his whistle for the GO signal, when a small white cat crept out on the road and started lapping up the milk. The whistle remained unblown, traffic stood still, and the light changed to green three times.

Only after the cat had drunk its fill and returned to the sidewalk did the patrolman give the signal for traffic to proceed.

Author Unknown

---

*Experience is not what happens to you;
it is what you do with what happens to you.*
ALDOUS HUXLEY

The Best Gift of All

A beautiful little girl was very sick and had to be confined to a hospital bed for quite some time. Since her family was very wealthy, they brought her the finest of toys—huge overstuffed animals, a variety of dolls with every imaginable change of dress, an ornate doll house, and the latest of games.

The little girl's mother was well known in social circles, and her face was often seen in the society columns at various charitable events. She brought something new every time she came to the hospital to visit her daughter. She never stayed very long, for she was always due at some luncheon or social gathering, but she never failed to bring a gift. The nurses and the doctors complained about the abundance of toys, games, and flowers that made it almost impossible for them to get around in the girl's room.

One day the little girl was particularly unhappy in the midst of all her fine gifts. Her mother was paying her daughter her usual short visit. The girl was desperately clinging to her mother, who tried to extricate herself so that she would not be late for a luncheon she was scheduled to attend that afternoon.

The mother tried to interest the child in a new and expensive doll that she had brought with her that day. "Mommy," cried the little girl, "I don't want another doll, I want *you*!" Surrounded by all the material things that a child could ever want, the girl desired the most important thing of all, her mother's presence.

Medard Laz

Loving Your Neighbor

I was home alone with the children: five-year-old David, three-year-old Karen, and Michael, the infant. My wife, Roe, was at work, her two-night-a-week position as a receptionist for an orthodontist. Just before dinner I realized that Karen had developed a high fever.

Perhaps I should take her to the doctor, I thought. Roe agreed, for I had called her at work for an opinion. After I hung up the phone, I walked out of the kitchen and found Karen slumped on the living-room couch. She was facing the ceiling and foaming at the mouth. Her eyes were rolled back. She was still and unconscious. I thought she was dying.

I didn't know what to do. Michael wasn't talking yet. David was bewildered. I simply wanted to run into the street and scream for help. I did scream: "Karen! Karen! Karen!" She wasn't responding.

The telephone. I called the police, the ambulance.

I rushed about through the dining room, through the living room, holding Karen, calling her name again and again, but there was still no response.

A minute later, I called the police again. "Please hurry!" Before I could place the receiver back in its place, the doorbell rang. Red and blue lights flashed throughout the neighborhood. I quickly answered the solid knocking, and there, standing before me, stood the tallest, broadest giant of a policeman I had ever seen. I could smell his leather coat. His shoes were shined. I wanted to hug him.

"I don't know what happened to my daughter! She isn't responding!"

"She's having a seizure," the policeman said in a low, confident voice. "Is she ill?"

"She has a fever! I know that! I was about to call the doctor!"

The policeman peacefully entered the house. "Let's take her upstairs and run some cool water in the bathtub. We need to bring her fever down a bit."

I pointed to the stairs. The policeman walked up, entered the bathroom, and began running the water. I was not aware that three or four neighbors had entered the house and were tending to David and Michael. I was not aware that the ambulance was on its way. All I knew was that a stranger was lifting my daughter out of my arms and gently placing her in a tepid tub of water.

I knelt on the floor to the left of the policeman. He, too, was kneeling and leaning over the wall of the bathtub, scooping up handsful of water and slowly pouring them over Karen's hot back. His gun was belted to his waist. His badge scraped against the porcelain. As he was tending to Karen, he turned to me and whispered, "I have a three-year-old daughter, too."

Karen began to respond. I dried her with a towel, dropped it on the floor, wrapped her in a wool blanket, and then carried her downstairs. My neighbors said they would watch over the boys. The ambulance drove onto the front lawn and right up to the front door. Two-way radios squawked in the background.

After I stepped into the ambulance through that wide, rear

door, I sat down and held Karen against my chest. I cried and cried.

The emergency room doctor said that Karen had suffered a febrile seizure, which some young children are prone to—a consultation with our family doctor was suggested. Her temperature dropped. Karen was fine.

In Tennessee Williams' play *The Glass Menagerie*, Amanda, the mother, tells her son, "We have to do all that we can to build ourselves up. In these trying times we live in, all that we have to cling to is each other."

After my daughter was safely tucked in bed that night, as I walked past the bathroom I noticed that our policeman had drained the bathtub and folded the towels.

This policeman, my policeman had no reason to be so kind, so interested, so caring, but like the good Samaritan, he stopped his regular routine and felt compassion for me and for my daughter.

Christopher de Vinck

Goodness is the only investment that never fails.
THOREAU

A Heart That Sings

A gust of winter air blasted in every time the sliding glass doors of the hospital opened. An elderly lady stood behind the doors and leaned heavily on her silver cane, looking expectantly out at the driveway.

I stood behind her waiting for my daughter, who had sprinted across the parking lot to get the car. We had been visiting my aunt, who was very ill.

Outside, a yellow cab was coming up the driveway. The woman's face brightened and she started out the door, saying, "Finally! I've waited so long." The cab pulled up, and just as it did, a middle-aged couple ran past me and the elderly lady, who was just approaching the cab. The couple jumped in and the cab sped off.

My daughter had seen the incident from her car. She rolled down her window and said, "Mom, ask her where she lives." The woman did not live very far from our destination.

She gratefully accepted the ride and related to us that her sister had been diagnosed with cancer. She had been with her all day.

When we dropped the woman off at her home, my daughter jumped out of the car, helped her up the walk, opened her door, and even carried the emptied garbage cans from the end of the driveway back to where they belonged.

I think nothing makes parents happier than to see the good works of their children. My heart sang that day.

Mary A. Hearn

Guest Appearance

I had just finished doing a seminar with speaker Florence Littauer in Texas. She had made a special point of reminding the audience, "Be alert to the people the Lord places around you, especially on airplanes."

This was a new thought for me. When I get on an airplane, I have two people in mind—the pilot and me. I am in deep prayer for both of us.

As I headed for the airport, I reminded myself to be alert.

The first leg of my flight was uneventful. Then we changed planes in Chicago, and I noticed an airline attendant helping to board an older woman in a wheelchair.

When my row was called, I found I was seated in front of the older woman. We each had an empty seat next to us. A few minutes later a young couple came down the aisle. They stopped at the row of the older woman.

The young woman looked at her ticket, looked at the number on the overhead panel, then leaned into the woman and said with contempt, "You're in my seat."

I turned around at this abruptness and saw the older lady shake her head and shrug her shoulders in an attempt to say "I don't understand."

When the woman shrugged, the younger gal announced for all to hear, "You're in my seat!"

I tried to defuse the situation by saying, "Excuse me, but I don't think she speaks English."

The younger woman turned on me and hissed, "I don't care what she speaks, I want her out of my seat." With that she called, "Stewardess."

Good, let the airlines handle her, I thought. I didn't want to deal with this traveling time bomb.

Usually flight personnel are trained to handle people problems. I think this attendant missed that class. She was almost as crude as the tactless traveler.

She looked down at the confused woman and demanded, "Let me see your tickets."

The older passenger realized this must be serious when she saw the attendant's uniform. Not understanding what they wanted, she gave her entire purse to the stewardess.

After rifling through her belongings, the flight gal found the ticket that verified the woman was in the wrong seat.

"Excuse me," I called to the attendant, "did you realize they boarded her in a wheelchair?"

"Really?" she whined, obviously annoyed. "This is going to make it harder to move her."

"Listen, why don't I move back there with her, and this... this... this couple can sit here," I said, pointing to my seat and the empty one beside me.

As I changed rows and took my new seat, I wanted this woman to know that all was well. I looked at her and smiled. She didn't respond.

Then I noticed she didn't have a seat belt on. I decided to help. It was a bigger job than I thought. I extended that belt as far as it would go, and it was prayer that closed it.

With that accomplished, I put on my belt, leaned back and closed my eyes. As the plane was taxiing for takeoff, I felt a hand on my hand. I turned and looked.

The older woman leaned over to me and slowly spoke the first words she had said, "You... first... Amer-i-can... be nice... to me."

Then taking her bracelet off her wrist, she pressed it into my hand and said, "I give you, you keep... OK?"

For a moment I couldn't respond. Then I swallowed the growing lump in my throat, slipped on the friendship bracelet and patted her hand. Her eyes filled with tears. My heart filled with gratitude.

Any room in your schedule for an unexpected guest?

Patsy Clairmont

Compassion is the chief law of human existence.
FYODOR DOSTOYEVSKY

Someone Who Cares

One day a grief-stricken mother sat in the visitor's lounge of a hospital. For her, the world had come to an end. She sobbed and sobbed as tears poured down from her eyes. She had been a single parent and now her daughter, her only child, had just died. The nurse on duty and the chaplain were trying to comfort her but her mind and her heart were light years away.

Outside the lounge, in the hallway next to her daughter's room, stood a forlorn little boy. His head was bowed and his eyes were shut. The nurse looked over and saw him standing there all by himself.

"Do you see that boy standing there in the hall?" said the nurse. Through her tears the mother looked into the hallway toward her daughter's room.

"Now there is a story," continued the nurse. "That little boy's mother is a young Serbian woman who was brought in here a week ago. They lost all of their family in the war and they came to this country four months ago with nothing but the clothes on their backs. They had been living in one shelter or another the whole time. They didn't know anyone in this country. They only had each other. Every day the boy has come and stood or sat there from morning until dark, in the vain hope that his mother would get better. She died about an hour ago. Now he has no one, not even a home to go back to."

The grieving mother was listening now. The nurse continued, "In a little bit I am going to have to go out and talk to that little boy and tell him that he now has no one in the whole world that he can call family." The nurse paused and looked plaintively at the woman next to her. She said hesitantly, "Would it at all be possible for you to go out there and tell him for me?"

The scene that took place at that moment was one that will forever be remembered by those who saw it. The woman stood up, wiped the tears from her eyes, composed herself, and went out into the hallway and put her arms around the little boy. She led that homeless child off with her to her childless home. In their own darkness, they became lights to each other.

Author Unknown

Don't ever let your problems become an excuse.
ANONYMOUS

How Tina Learned She Was Loved

How does it feel to be eight years old and not wanted by your parents? Most of us will never know. But Tina knows.

The day the caseworker brought Tina for a visit, my husband and I were nervous. But when I saw the anxiety in her big blue eyes, my nervousness gave way to sympathy. How does it feel to be a child who has to talk with strangers to find a suitable home?

We sat like statues in our living room while her eyes wandered to our two dogs, the trees outside the window, and the ceiling that needed painting. When asked if she had any questions, she looked me straight in the eye. "Do you have any other boyfriends?" Now there's a question I don't hear every day. When I assured her that I was happy with just Jim, she turned to him.

"Do you get drunk very much?" How does it feel to be a child and see strange men brought home by your mother and eventually see your father, raving drunk, shoot one of them before your eyes?

Luckily for us, we met with Tina's approval, and she moved in on an unforgettable Friday. Our daughter Beth was home from college for the occasion and was looking forward to meeting her little sister. Would three o'clock ever come? I dusted things that didn't need dusting, Jim fixed things that didn't need fixing, and Beth almost brushed the dogs bald.

At last the car pulled into the driveway. We dashed out, the dogs at our heels. Tina climbed out of the car, gingerly carrying all her worldly possessions in a cardboard box. Both dogs gleefully jumped all over her, and made her drop her package. All of us began to pick up the scattered clothing. Then I looked at Tina. She had both thin arms across her face, and was sobbing softly and whimpering. "I didn't mean to drop it. Please don't hit me."

My heart sank. I'd never seen real fear and utter misery in a child's eyes before.

"Of course you didn't, honey," Beth said, and tried to put her arms around her. Tina pulled away, picked up the filled box, and headed toward the house.

Realizing how sad her life had been, we went all out to make her like us and our home. I cooked her favorite foods, and Jim catered to her every whim. In trying to build up her confidence, we inadvertently let her get by with childish pranks we'd never tolerated from Beth at her age.

Most of the time Tina was polite, sometimes overly so. Evidently, she did like us and didn't want to take any chances of our shipping her out. If your own mother deserts you, what can you expect from strangers?

One day she asked, "If I get really sick in the middle of the night, what can I do?" When assured she could call on me, she looked skeptical. "Don't you and Daddy Jim go out after I go to sleep?" How does it feel to be younger than eight, wake up sick, and find you're on you're own?

The first few months with Tina were filled with many trials and mixed emotions. She was well behaved on the whole, but she didn't show us any affection and was leery if we got too close to her. She seemed almost to worship the dogs, though, and had long conversations with them. I even broke down and let Trixie, the little poodle, sleep at the foot of Tina's bed. Usually, she was in Tina's bed by morning.

The episode that changed our relationship with Tina was a special, odd kind of miracle. One Saturday afternoon, when I went out for the newspaper, I heard car brakes screech and a man yell. I looked up in time to see Tina swerve on her bike, laugh at the driver, and dare him to hit her. I saw red.

I grabbed a good, keen branch from the closest tree and marched Tina into the house, switching her legs as we went. I ordered her to bed.

She cried. Great, heaving sobs in total abandonment. This was the first time I'd ever known her really to cry, as a child cries. Once she'd caught her fingers in the car door and didn't utter a sound; she just pulled her lips tightly together and wrung her hands. It was so unnatural, it gave me an eerie feeling. (Later I learned that Tina had been beaten for crying.)

I made her supper as I cursed myself for being so cross with her and actually switching her legs. After all, this child had been through hell and wasn't responsible for the outlandish ways she had of demanding attention. I was full of pity for her and disgust with myself.

The supper tray held all her favorites: hot dog, potato chips, cookies, and a big milkshake. I'd apologize and try to make right what I'd done.

Tina looked at me with red, swollen eyes. "Will you stay with me while I eat?" For once in my life I had sense enough to keep my mouth shut and only say, "Yes, I'll get myself a cup of coffee."

After eating like a football player, she peered at me apprehensively and said: "I think I deserved that spanking. But I didn't think you'd really do it!"

Apology forgotten, I took my cue. "Well, I did, honey. And I will again, anytime it's necessary. Jim and I love you, and it would break our hearts if you were badly hurt."

She stared at me unbelievingly, but wanting so hard to believe. I added, "And that's not the whole point. The poor man driving that car was scared out of his wits. He didn't want to hit you. His feelings count, too. You and I are not the only ones with feelings."

"Bozo and Trixie have feelings, too," she said. Then she actually grinned! "I love you and Beth and Daddy Jim, too," she said.

"And we love you," I replied, feeling as though I'd burst.

Tina is older now. She's never been physically punished since that day when she was eight. She has been sent to her room, curtailed in her activities, and talked to, sometimes quite loudly. She's a typical child; sweet, unpredictable, idealistic, and knows far more than any of the elderly set.

How does it feel to be a child and know you're loved and essential to a close family circle? Now Tina knows.

Author Unknown

Learning to Talk

In Australia, I went to an arthritis camp for children, and among the children was this six-year-old girl, Victoria, who was very seriously ill with arthritis. Her parents had flown her down from Darwin to this camp, but Victoria wouldn't even speak; she just sat huddled up in a little wheelchair. So, I got her out of her wheelchair and onto my lap, you see? I tried to involve her, asked her questions, but nothing, nothing. "She never speaks," her mother said.

Then I started to lead the other children in a sing-along. Some time ago I'd made an LP record of me singing children's songs, including "Old MacDonald Had a Farm." All the kids joined me in that song but Victoria. We were all making animal noises—you know them!—and when we got to the pig, I put the microphone up to Victoria, and she went "honk, honk!" Marvelous! Lovely! She sat straight up! So, from then on, no matter what the animal was, every time I put the mike up to Victoria she would "honk, honk."

We finished the song, and the next thing I know she's smiling. I say to her, "O, come on, Victoria, what's it like in Darwin?" And she starts telling me about her family. It was fantastic! It was lovely! If I didn't ever do anything else in my life, that was one of the great experiences.

David Prowse

The first duty of love is to listen.
PAUL TILLICH

Belonging

With the freeway ahead of us and home behind, the photographer and I left on a three-day newspaper assignment. We were bound for the Columbia Gorge, where the Columbia River carves a mile-wide path between Washington and Oregon; where windsurfers come from across the country to dance across waves created by "nuclear winds"; where I would be far away from the world of nine-to-five and deadlines and routines and errands and rushing kids to baseball practices and having to make sure my socks weren't left on the bedroom floor.

Far away from the R word—responsibility.

Frankly, it had not been the perfect farewell. Our family was running on empty. Our '81 car was showing signs of automotive Alzheimer's. We were all tired, cranky, trying to shake colds.

My eight-year-old son tried to perk us up with his off-key version of a song from the musical, *Annie:*

The sun will come out tomorrow;
bet your bottom dollar that tomorrow there'll be sun.

It didn't work. I had been busy trying to get ready for the trip; my wife Sally had been busy fretting because my three days of freedom were going to cost her three days of extra responsibility.

"Daddy, are you coming to hear my class sing Thursday night?" Jason, my eight-year-old, asked amid the chaos of my departure.

Had I been Bill Cosby, I would have gotten a funny expression on my face, said "Well, of course," and everyone would have lived happily ever after—or at least for a half an hour.

But I didn't feel much like Bill Cosby that morning. "I'm going to be out of town," I said. "Sorry."

Giving Sally a quick kiss, I was on my way. Now, hours later, I was far away from family, free from the clutter, the runny noses, the demands on my time.

Knowing little about each other, the photographer and I shared a bit about ourselves as we drove. Roughly my age—mid-30's—he was married but had no children. He and his wife had seen too many situations where couples with children had found themselves strapped down, scurrying for babysitters and forced to give up spontaneous trips.

He told me how he and his wife had recently taken a trip to the Gorge by themselves. My mind did a double take. *By themselves?* What was that like? Long ago, in a universe far, far away, I vaguely remembered what that was like. Taking off when the mood hit. No pleas for horseback rides about the time you're ready to crash for the night. No tornado-swept rooms. No meet-the-teacher nights.

Besides having no children, the photographer had no six-month-old French fries on the floor of his car, no legs of Superman action figures on his dashboard and no road maps on which most of Idaho had been obliterated by a melted Snickers bar.

Where had I gone wrong?

For the next couple of days, despite a threat of rain, we

explored the Gorge—thousand-foot-walls of basalt rising on either side of the Columbia, fluorescent-clad sailboarders, like neon gnats, carving wakes in the water.

If the land and water were intriguing, so were the windsurfers. There were thousands of them, nearly all of them baby boomers, spending their days on the water, their nights on the town, their mornings in bed.

Every fourth car had a board on top. License plates from all over the country dotted the streets. Some of these "board-heads" were follow-the-wind free spirits who lived out of the back of vans; others were well-established yuppies who were here for a weekend or vacation.

In the evenings, the river's hub town turned into Oregon's version of a California beach town: boomers eating, drinking, and being merry, lost in a world of frivolity and freedom.

For me, seeing this group was like discovering a lost, ancient tribe. You mean, while I was busy trying to put on jammed bike chains, these people were jamming to the rock beat of dance clubs? While I was depositing paychecks to be spent on groceries and orthodontic bills and college funds, these people were deciding what color sailboards to buy?

Where had I gone wrong?

On our last night, the cloudy weather continued, which irked the photographer and mirrored the mood that had overcome me; we both needed sunshine, only for different reasons. As I stared from the motel room at the river below, I felt a sort of emptiness, as if I didn't belong. Not here. Not home. Not anywhere. Just as the winds of the Gorge were whipping the river into whitecaps, so were the winds of freedom buffeting my beliefs. Faith. Marriage. Children. Work. I had anchored my life on such things, and yet now found myself slipping from that fixed position. Had I made a mistake? Had I sold out to the rigors of responsibility? Someday, when I was older, would I suddenly face the brittle-cold reality of regret, wishing I had gone with the wind?

I was getting ready for bed when I spotted it—a card in my suitcase, buried beneath some clothes. It was from Sally. The card featured cows—my wife's big on bovines—and simply said, "I'll love you till the cows come home."

I stared at the card for minutes. I repeated the words. I looked at the same handwriting that I'd seen on love letters in college, on a marriage certificate, on two birth certificates, on a will. As I went to bed, there was no need to call the front desk and ask for a wake-up call; I'd already gotten one. The card bored through my hardened heart, convicted my selfish conscience, refocused my blurry perspective. I knew exactly where I needed to be.

The next day, after a two-hour interview, six-hour drive and three-block sprint, I arrived at my son's school, anxious and out of breath. The singing program had started twenty minutes before; had I missed Jason's song?

I rushed into the cafeteria. It was jammed. Almost frantically, I weaved my way through a crowd of parents clogging the entrance, to where I could finally get a glimpse of the kids on stage. That's when I heard them: twenty-five first-grade voices trying desperately to hit notes that were five years away.

The sun will come out tomorrow;
bet your bottom dollar that tomorrow there'll be sun.

My eyes searched this collage of kids, looking for Jason. Finally, I spotted him. Front row, as usual, squished between a couple of girls whose germs, judging by the look on his face, were crawling over him like picnic ants. He was singing, all right, but with less enthusiasm than when he's been told to clean his room.

Suddenly, his eyes shifted my way and his face lit up with the kind of smile a father only gets to see in a grade-school singing program when his eyes meet his child's. He had seen me, a moment that will forever stay frozen in my memory.

Later, through a sea of faces, I caught sight of Sally and my other son. After the program, amid a mass of parent-child humanity, the four of us rendezvoused, nearly oblivious to the commotion surrounding us. I felt no emptiness, only connectedness.

How could one man be so blessed?

In the days to come, I resumed my part in life as a bike-fixer and breadwinner, husband and father, roles that would cause a windsurfer to yawn. But for all the excitement of riding the wind, I decided, I'll take the front-row smile of my eight-year-old son. And for all the freedom of life in the Gorge, I'll take the responsibility of caring for the woman who vowed to love me till the cows come home.

Bob Welch

How You Play the Game

It was New Year's Day. Penn State was squared off against Alabama in the Sugar Bowl to determine who was number one in college football. Most observers felt that Penn State should have won the game. But they had a touchdown called back because of a stupid penalty—Penn State had a twelfth man on the field.

In the locker room after the game, Joe Paterno, the legendary coach of Penn State, was asked to identify the player who caused the penalty and probably cost them the national championship. "It's only a game," Paterno said. "I have no intention of ever identifying the boy. He just made a mistake."

Author Unknown

It's not a question of who's going to throw the first stone; it's a question of who's going to start building with it.
Sloan Wilson

The Return

There was a small dog who had been struck by a car and was lying by the side of the road. A doctor was driving by and he noticed the dog and he saw that he was still alive. He stopped his car, picked up the dog, and took him home with him. There he discovered that the dog had been mostly stunned as a result of the accident. After a careful examination the doctor concluded that the animal had suffered a few minor cuts and abrasions, but was otherwise all right.

He revived the dog, cleaned up the wounds, and was carrying the animal from the house to the garage. All of a sudden the dog jumped from his arms and scampered off in an instant. "What an ungrateful little dog," the doctor said to himself. "After all that I have done for you!"

He did not give the incident a second thought until the next evening when he heard a scratching at the door. He could not imagine who it was. When he opened the door, there was the little dog he had treated accompanied by another hurt dog.

Author Unknown

A kind deed receives compound interest.
ANONYMOUS

A Nest of Kindness

An apple farmer pruned his orchard, and as he did he made a big pile of branches away from all his buildings. One morning he noted a bird with its beak full of materials, starting to make a nest in that heap of prunings. Returning that way at sundown, he reached into the pile and tore the nest apart. The bird flew around, chirping wildly, as if to say, "You cruel man!"

The next day the farmer saw the bird again trying to build a nest at another place but in the same pile. Again that night he destroyed all the labor the bird had expended. The bird's wild flutterings and chirpings seemed to say, "How terrible you are to destroy my nest!"

The third day the farmer noticed that the bird was building in a rose bush quite a distance from the pile of prunings. This time the farmer simply smiled and let the bird alone.

Soon eggs appeared in the nest, then fledglings. But before the tiny birds were old enough to leave the nest, the farmer completed his work in the orchard. As he had intended all along, the farmer burned the piles of pruned branches to the ground. Because the mother bird had moved her nest to the rose bushes, the baby birds were unharmed by the fire.

Author Unknown

Goodness is the only investment that never fails.
HENRY DAVID THOREAU

It's My Bag

I keep my bag right with me everywhere I go,
In case I might need to wear it, so ME doesn't show.
I'm so afraid to show you ME, afraid of what you'll do.
You might laugh at ME, or say mean things....
Or I might lose you.
I'd like to take my bag off, to let you look at ME.
I want you to try to understand, and please,
    love what you see.
So, if you'll be patient and close your eyes,
    I'll pull it off so slow.
Please understand how much it hurts, to let the real ME
    show.
Now my bag is taken off. I feel naked! Bare! So cold!
If you still love all that you see, you are my friend,
    pure as gold.
I want to save my bag, and hold it in my hand.
I need to keep it handy in case someone doesn't understand.
Please protect ME, my new friend.
Thank you for loving ME true.
But, please let me keep my bag with me until I love ME, too.

Author Unknown

---

*Most people believe they see the world as it is.
However, we really see the world as we are.*
ANONYMOUS

THREE

LOVE ADDS *a* LITTLE CHOCOLATE... TO UNDERSTANDING

Love is not blind—
it sees more, not less.
But because it sees more,
it is willing to see less.
RABBI JULIUS GORDON

I Have Permission to
Pay Attention to Myself

It seems that some folks pay attention to nothing else. Their lives are bordered on the north, south, east, and west by... self... and that's all. They remind me of the man who prayed thus: "Bless me and my wife, our son, John, and his wife; us four and no more. Amen."

Most of us who get cancer, though, aren't like that. We're "pretty good people." We work hard. We feel guilty if we don't get things done. We blame ourselves if things go wrong. We feel that we have to make the world a better place. We're embarrassed if we're not "making a difference." For people like us, any attention at all to our selves is "selfishness."

Besides, we really are busy. We have jobs and families and friends and organizations. The whole world conspires to jam us in traffic and never to be there when we telephone and to get in line in front of us in the supermarket. There's just no time for self! We've got cars that are past their oil change mileage and toilets that are fighting back and children who are tugging at our legs and... Even in those spare moments when we look wistfully toward the unread books and recall the times we prayed or meditated, there's no time to follow up.

So we've become machines instead of people, robots rather than persons, lists instead of lovers, date books rather than selves.

Now, however, there's a clearing in the forest. It's burnt over harshly, down to the stubble, but it's still a clearing. It gives me a chance to see a wider view, a vision of the sky.

Now it's OK for me to take the time to visualize, to pray, to read, to nap, to sit, to stare, to meditate… to be.

A man dies and we hear someone ask, "What was he worth?" "Oh, probably half a million," someone answers. Half a million what? Embraces? Prayers? Loves? Kindnesses? Sunsets? Bird songs? Walks? Meals with friends? "Of course not! Half a million *dollars*!" Is that all someone is worth? Dollars? If it's dollars, then it doesn't make any difference whether it's five or five billion. The same is true with all the other events and activities by which we usually measure worth. Did she make vice president? So what? Was he the star? Big deal. A forty-year pin? Big whoop!

It's not what you *do* but what you *are*! That's where this business of self comes in. My life has meaning not because I'm acceptable, but because I'm accepted, not because I'm lovable, but because I'm loved. I'm a part of Life, a child of God. I *am*! I'm not a statistical summary—worked thirty years, married once, fathered two, made some bucks, watched some TV.

So now that I have cancer, it's OK just to be. Somehow I have permission from myself and the rest of the world to concentrate on this self, in order to get well. In the process, I have a chance not just to get cured, but to get whole, to be who I'm meant to be.

John Robert McFarland

The Goodness Within

One day a beggar was out in front of the commuter station in a major city. He stopped a lawyer who was headed for the evening train and asked him for a quarter. As the lawyer reached into his pocket to give the beggar some change, he took a long, hard look into the man's unshaven face. The attorney asked him, "Don't I know you from somewhere?"

"You should," responded the disheveled man. "I'm your former classmate from Bridgemont. Remember, Cahill Hall?"

"Why, Gerry, now I remember you! Gosh, it's got to be over twenty years ago." Without any further discussion the lawyer wrote a check for $1,000. "Here, take this and make a new start. No matter what has happened in the past, it's the future that counts. Good luck." With that the lawyer hurried off to catch his train.

Thoughts of years past and happier times flooded the poor man's mind as he walked to the bank that was nearby. When he arrived he stopped at the door and immediately grew frightened. He saw through the glass doors the well-dressed tellers and the spotlessly clean interior. Then he looked at his own filthy rags reflected in the mirror of the lobby. "They won't cash this for me. They'll swear that I forged it," Gerry muttered as he turned away and headed back to the poor side of town.

The next day the two men met again in front of the station. The lawyer got right to the point. "Why Gerry, it seems that nothing has changed for you. What did you do with my check?" asked the lawyer. "Gamble it away, drink it up?"

"No," said the beggar. He pulled the check out of his dirty shirt pocket and handed it back to his benefactor, explaining why he hadn't cashed it. The lawyer stared at the piece of paper in his hands for a moment as the man slowly walked away. Determined to help his old friend, the attorney ran after the man and personally escorted him to the bank, assuring him kindly:

"Go on in, my friend. You'll see. What matters is not your appearance, but my signature."

Author Unknown

Everything in life is most fundamentally a gift. And you receive it best and you live it best by holding it with very open hands.
LEO O'DONOVAN

Pets Have the Answer

Our little poodle, Tinker, has become a big part of our lives. He hardly ever goes outdoors, sleeps in whatever bed he chooses, lies on his favorite living room chair, and spends a lot of time on the back of the couch looking out the big picture window. There is always food and water in his special dishes, and he is loaded with toys. He certainly does not want for love. He has made his way into our hearts and very well knows it. In other words, he is in charge of the house and allows us to live in it.

The day my mother-in-law moved in with us, she brought her cat, Penelope. When Tinker first saw Penelope, he barked loudly, growled a little, and then ran under the bed. He would not come out from under the bed, even to eat. He lost weight and was not his usual self anymore. Once in a while he would venture out into the living room, and instantly Penelope would spring forth, ready to get acquainted. Tinker would growl and bark at her and run under the bed.

Penelope never gave up on becoming friends with Tinker. Whenever she got a chance, she'd go toward Tinker in a hopeful way, and Tinker would just growl, bark, and run.

Finally Tinker relented and stayed out from under the bed, but he still growled and barked a lot. Nevertheless, Penelope was excited and watched Tinker's every move, careful not to venture too close. Tinker would look back at Penelope with narrowed eyes and growl with his leave-me-alone warning.

But very slowly Penelope got Tinker to come closer, by pretending to be asleep. One day I caught them eating together. Another day they were both sleeping in Tinker's favorite chair. Tinker finally stopped growling and barking.

Too often, I'm like Tinker. I pout when I think of someone else getting the love and affection I deserve. How much better it would be if I were like Penelope, who never worries about how much she deserves but instead concerns herself with how much love she can give.

Carol Goll Burris

Happiness is like a cat. If you try to coax it or call it,
it will avoid you; it will never come.
But if you pay no attention to it and go about your business,
you'll find it rubbing against your leg and jumping into your lap.
WILLIAM BENNETT

She Thinks I'm Real!

A waitress was taking orders from a couple and their young son. She was one of the class of veteran waitresses who never show outright disrespect to their customers, but who frequently make it quietly evident by their unhurried pace and their level stare that they fear no mortal, not even parents. She jotted on her pad deliberately and silently as the father and mother gave their selection and gratuitous instructions as to what was to be substituted for what, and which dressing changed to what sauce.

When she finally turned to the boy, he began his order with a kind of fearful desperation. "I want a hot dog—," he started. And both parents barked at once, "No hot dog!" The mother went on. "Bring him the lyonnaise potatoes and the beef, both vegetables, and a hard roll and—"

The waitress wasn't even listening. She said evenly to the youngster, "What do you want on your hot dog?" He flashed an amazed smile.

"Ketchup, lots of ketchup, and—bring a glass of milk."

"Coming up," she said as she turned from the table, leaving behind her the stunned silence of utter parental dismay. The boy watched her go before he turned to his father and mother with astonished elation to say, "You know what? She thinks I'm real! She thinks I'm real!"

Frederick B. Speakman

When Social Security Speaks

"I'm sorry, Ms. Senter. We cannot issue you a new driver's license without verification of your social security number." For the third time I patiently try to explain that I don't have a social security card anymore. It was stolen at the train station along with my driver's license, wallet, credit cards, bank cards, cash, and children's pictures.

Isn't it bad enough that I have to be here today, fighting traffic, facing long, irritating lines of people who would rather be anywhere but here? I take a number and wait my turn, only to be told, "The computers are down at this facility today, but you may obtain a license at another Secretary of State's office, ten miles east, right off the 290 Expressway." And all for crimes I didn't commit. I am still chafing at the thought that some stranger, pushing through post-Christmas rush at Union Station, would have the nerve to zip open my purse and steal my wallet. The inconvenience of it all has not been made any easier today when I arrive here, only to find that I have to keep driving—first to a town thirty minutes away to obtain a social security clearance, and then another half hour to a second facility where, hopefully, the computers are functioning.

As though I have nothing better to do with my time, I mutter to myself as I take a number and join a third line, this one at the social security office. I sense that this is not a happy place to be. Toddlers whine. Adults complain. Being reduced to a number seems to have drained those of us who wait of any semblance of goodwill and peaceful understanding.

"Never have I seen such a rude place in all my life," an old man with a leathery face laments as he pounds his cane on the tile floor. "Have to take a number before they will even answer your question." He addresses his comments to no one in particular, but we all nod in silent accord. The cold efficiency, the impersonality of it all does not sit well with me either, especially when I know there is more to come after I leave this place.

And all because someone had the nerve to steal my wallet. I return to the source of my misery and feel my jaw tighten again. I have gone through the scenario before. An unguarded moment. Divided attention. Rushing crowd around me. And how often have I reminded my teenage daughter to carry her purse in front of her when she's in a crowd. I do not easily forgive myself or the thief.

I am still bothered and disturbed, not only by the theft, but by the hassles of the day, when my number is called and I step to the counter. I am aware that someone in a pink coat steps up beside me. I am also aware that it is not her turn. *I sat and waited. Let her do the same*, I think to myself.

"I'm sorry, miss, you'll have to take a number and wait your turn." The clerk speaks the irritation I feel.

"But all I needed was..." Two small children pull at her coat, and the baby in her arms cries a hacking cry. The clerk repeats her instructions with growing force and irritation.

"Please, ma'am," the young mother starts again. This time her words come out with a sob. "All I wanted to know... is this where I get my husband's death certificate?"

We are stopped short, the clerk and I. Neither of us knows

what to say. I want to gather the mother into my arms, wipe away her tears, hold her crying baby, calm her restless toddlers. Instead I step back from the counter and mumble something about being sorry and, "Go ahead." The clerk speaks to the grieving woman in hushed tones, then hands me the necessary forms, and I return to my seat to write. But I have been silenced and humbled. *A lost wallet, and she has lost a husband,* I reflect as I fill out the forms. My losses seemed tragic until now.

I drive to my next stop with a thankful heart. In my mind, I see the woman in the pink coat again and hear her sob. And even as I drive, I pray about her loss and begin the process of forgetting my own.

Ruth Senter

When the satisfaction or the security of another person becomes as significant to one as one's own security, then the state of love exists.
HENRY STACK SULLIVAN

Snatching a Victory
in the Final Moments

~♥~

I watched a football game not too long ago between the Cardinals and the Cowboys. The Cardinals were two touchdowns behind. Their offense managed only a field goal against the Cowboys during the first fifty-eight minutes of play. Yet, launching into their final two-minute drill, the Cardinals scored three touchdowns and won the game.

However improbable, this reversal doesn't hold a candle to that of a man I knew. With far more than a game hanging in the balance, his own "two-minute drill" was nothing less than miraculous. With time running out, he recovered his old fumbles and scored a victory in death that had eluded him for a lifetime.

The old man was dying, and so he summoned his children to his bedside to tell them good-bye. Dutifully they assembled, apprehensive less because of his impending death than of his forbidding life. With family members related to one another by bonds of mutual estrangement, feelings had been strained for years, muted by pretense, insulated by formality.

In times past, whenever the old man had engaged members of his family in serious conversation, he had managed to direct the subject to his will. He seemed to think of his children and grandchildren principally as beneficiaries. They addressed him as "Sir." Always proper, he was like a silk glove on an iron fist, one of those people for whom it would have been much easier to write an obituary than a eulogy. His accomplishments were many, but all in the public domain: a brilliant business career, success in government service, renown as a philanthropist. Respected by all who knew him, feared by many, and loved by none, he served humanity through his industry and generosity, yet apparently had no inclination to establish intimacy with anyone. None of those who remember his late, stately wife recall ever having seen the two of them touch, even accidentally. But now he was dying, and one by one he called his children to him.

"John, I have not given you the respect nor shown you the love that you deserve. I know how much this hurt you, though you never seem to show it. In that respect, you are just like your dad. But in other ways, you've far outstripped me. Please know that I am prouder of you, and all the things you have done, than I am of my own accomplishments.

"Dorothy, when your mother died, a part of me died with her. The pain was so great that I retreated in self-protection from everyone I loved. Probably because you are so like her, I retreated from you most of all. I never had the strength to tell you. If only Mother and I had given you a glimpse of how deeply we loved each other, so many of your problems might have been avoided. I'm sorry. I love you.

"Billy, I know you have rejected all the things I seem to value—position, money, status in society. You won't believe this, but I almost did the same thing myself when I was your age. But I didn't have the courage. Please don't let anyone force you to be someone you are not. To me, you will always be the man I might have been."

Then the old man called the whole family together, addressing all the rest of them, each in turn. He took out a thick book of clippings and letters, filled with his grandchildren's accomplishments, their wedding pictures, academic awards, and stories recounting triumphs on the athletic field. Who could have imagined how deeply he cared? Leafing through it page by page, he told them each how proud he was.

As the evening went on, they began to exchange stories, laughing together, and crying a bit too, in relief as much as pain. He told them tales of his youth, especially of his deep passion and devotion to their mother and grandmother. Then he kissed them each good-bye. They returned to their homes. He died a short time later. As one friend told me, "The old man finally accomplished in death something that eluded him in life. He brought his family together."

As the saying goes, "In life, as in football, the score at half-time doesn't matter." It may not be fair, and the odds may be long against it happening, but all it takes to turn a bad game around is a spectacular "two-minute drill."

E. Forrester Church

It is the highest creatures who take the longest to mature, and are the most helpless during their immaturity.
G. B. SHAW

The Ladder Test

My childhood home on Orchard Street was set in a small town in the rolling hills of northern New Jersey. It was a three-story, mint-green stucco affair with forest-green shutters and a shingled roof that was in constant need of repair. Money was tight, and so my father did the repairs himself at night and on weekends. However, when my sisters and I grew into our teens, the roof served another purpose: my father used it to gauge the character of the young men who came to call.

The first time a prospective suitor came to the house, Dad would go outside just before the "guinea pig" arrived, propping his extension ladder against the side of the house. Laying a hammer at the foot of the ladder, my father would then climb up and pretend to work. When the boy pulled up, Dad good-naturedly called out:

"Hey, there! Dropped my hammer. Could you toss it up to me?"

Had the boy refused to get out of his car, I'm certain the date would have been over. (Fortunately, we all had better sense than to invite someone like that home in the first place.) However, if he picked up the hammer, climbed the ladder partway, and tossed it to my father (as requested), the young man got a single "star." That was enough for a single date, but not enough for him to be considered a serious contender for our affections.

If the young man climbed the ladder, handed the tool to Dad, and engaged him in a bit of lighthearted banter, that was better: two stars. Enough for a second date. A real conversation earned a guy three stars—and the respect of my father.

One of my boyfriends, a handy young man, was so eager to please that he climbed up and proceeded to spend the afternoon helping Dad tear shingles off the roof, leaving me to stew dateless in the kitchen. Later Dad tried to smooth my ruffled feathers by exclaiming over the young man's sterling character. I could "keep this one" if I wanted to, he said. (I didn't, but have always regretted it.) My sister's friend John helped my father put the finishing touches on the roof—and he later became my brother-in-law.

The roof completed, my parents sold the house and moved to another state. My younger sisters didn't have the benefit of "The Ladder Test," and I can't help but wonder if all our lives would have been easier had Dad found another roof to fix. Flowers are sweet, and candy is dandy—but nothing says "keeper" to a girl like a guy who's willing to face her father armed with nothing but a hammer.

Heidi Hess

We can do no great things;
only small things with great love.
MOTHER TERESA

Seeing the Light

My neighbor casually broke the news. We were out in our yards chatting in typical fashion over the back fence. She glanced up at the majestic old tree towering above us on her side of the property line. "You know, Joe's going to see about having this taken down," she told me.

The tree? My mind raced. The tree I've stared into all these years from the window over my kitchen sink? The one that provides blessed shade in the heat of a summer?

"Oh," was all I could manage.

My expression must have given me away.

"I know," she said sympathetically. "We hate to do it. But after that last windstorm..."

I nodded agreement, recalling that frightening episode. A huge limb had come crashing down, landing with a thud that shook the ground. Miraculously, it missed both our houses.

Cleaning up the supper dishes that night, I sadly watched a pair of squirrels performing their aerial act high in the branches. They're gonna miss their tree, I thought.

A few days later, a truck pulled up in front of my neighbor's house. Strong young men armed with ropes and chainsaws began their assault on the tree.

At first, I watched in horrified fascination as limb after limb was sawed off and lowered to the ground. It's only a tree, I chided myself, as I turned away with a heavy heart.

When I looked again, all that remained was an ugly stump. In a few days, they returned to grind that down, obliterating all traces of the once proud tree.

I confessed my sense of loss to an older friend. "The yard looks so bare now," I said forlornly.

"You'll get used to it," she said, trying to console me. "The thing is not to dwell on what you lost, but on how much you have left."

"I know," I said, the way you do when you're unconvinced, but trying to be polite.

My days settled into their familiar pattern. But, then I began to notice things. My kitchen, which had never been dim, was now brighter than ever, flooded with sunlight. I found I hardly ever needed the light over my kitchen sink anymore.

My unobstructed view allowed me to see all the way through to the next block. I watched the children walking home from school, laughing and shouting; I spotted the mail carrier on his rounds.

Next spring it will be time to plan a new garden. I almost feel guilty anticipating the wonderful tomatoes I'll be able to grow with all that extra sun.

Suddenly, my friend's wise words came to mind. I must call, and let her know I now understand she was talking about more than the loss of a tree. I really do have so much to appreciate.

Anne Drucker

Will You Share the Light?

Long ago, or maybe not so long ago, there was a tribe in a dark, cold cavern.

The cave dwellers would huddle together and cry against the chill. Loud and long they wailed. It was all they did. It was all they knew how to do. The sounds in the cave were mournful, but the people didn't know it, for they had never known joy. The spirit in the cave was death, but the people didn't know it, for they had never known life.

But then, one day, they heard a different voice. "I have heard your cries," it announced. "I have felt your chill and seen your darkness. I have come to help."

The cave people grew quiet. They had never heard this voice. Hope sounded strange to their ears. "How can we know you have come to help?"

"Trust me," he answered. "I have what you need."

The cave people peered through the darkness at the figure of the stranger. He was stacking something, then stooping and stacking more.

"What are you doing?" one cried, nervous.

The stranger didn't answer.

"What are you making?" one shouted even louder.

Still no response.

"Tell us!" demanded a third.

The visitor stood and spoke in the direction of the voices. "I have what you need." With that he turned to the pile at his feet and lit it. Wood ignited, flames erupted, and light filled the cavern.

The cave people turned away in fear. "Put it out!" they cried. "It hurts to see it."

"Light always hurts before it helps," he answered. "Step closer. The pain will soon pass."

"Not I," declared a voice.

"Nor I," agreed a second.

"Only a fool would risk exposing his eyes to such light."

The stranger stood next to the fire. "Would you prefer the darkness? Would you prefer the cold? Don't consult your fears. Take a step of faith."

For a long time no one spoke. The people hovered in groups covering their eyes. The fire builder stood next to the fire. "It's warm here," he invited.

"He's right," one from behind him announced. "It's warmer." The stranger turned and saw a figure slowly stepping toward the fire, "I can open my eyes now," she proclaimed. "I can see."

"Come closer," invited the fire builder.

She did. She stepped into the ring of light. "It's so warm!" She extended her hands and sighed as her chill began to pass.

"Come, everyone! Feel the warmth," she invited.

"Silence, woman!" cried one of the cave dwellers. "Dare you lead us into your folly? Leave us. Leave us and take your light with you."

She turned to the stranger. "Why won't they come?"

"They choose the chill, for though it's cold, it's what they know. They'd rather be cold than change."

"And live in the dark?"

"And live in the dark."

The now-warm woman stood silent. Looking first at the dark, then at the man.

"Will you leave the fire?" he asked.

She paused, then answered, "I cannot. I cannot bear the cold." Then she spoke again. "But nor can I bear the thought of my people in darkness."

"You don't have to," he responded, reaching into the fire and removing a stick. "Carry this to your people. Tell them the light is here, and the light is warm. Tell them the light is for all who desire it."

And she took the small flame and stepped into the shadows.

Max Lucado

The only limits are, as always, those of vision.
JAMES BROUGHTON

Looking at You

Looking at you
  I see
  a mirror image
  of myself
  turned inside out

The other side of my coin
  the one I can't see
  alone
  by myself
The one I come to know
  in myself
  only through seeing it
  first reflected
  from outside myself

I need you.

Susan M. Campbell

*Love is but the discovery of ourselves in others and
the delight in the recognition.*
ALEXANDER SMITH

FOUR

LOVE ADDS a LITTLE CHOCOLATE... TO THE FAMILY

Some children were asked, "What is love?"
One little girl answered, "Love is when your
mommy reads you a bedtime story.
True love is when she doesn't skip any pages."
AUTHOR UNKNOWN

PEANUTS reprinted by permission of United Features Syndicate, Inc.

Mothers of the Bride

The two women are as different as could be. One is petite, with carefully coiffed blonde-gray hair that moves in gentle waves around her face. Her youthful-looking form is dressed in a tasteful, winter-white, mother-of-the-bride dress. Her face glows with pride over her newlywed daughter.

The woman's name is Marilyn, and she is my adoptive mother. She beams at me, the child she cherished and raised for 28 years, even though she didn't give birth to me.

The other woman stops just inside the door of the reception hall. She wears a red and blue dress with a longish sweater top that covers a rather round form. A black wig surrounds her cheerful, ruddy face, more ravaged by time than the other woman's, though she is actually younger.

She has shaved her eyebrows and drawn them back in with a pencil—a makeup trick that long-ago fashion magazines recommended. Her round cheeks are heavily but carefully rouged. She has prepared herself for a very important event.

Her face is filled with pride, but something else, too: she is nervous. So nervous. She is preparing to meet the family to whom she relinquished her infant daughter such a long time ago. A family of people she has agonized about for nearly half of her life—always wondering, hoping they were strong and good and that she had made the right decision.

The woman's name is Dorothy, and she is my birth mother.

From across the reception hall I see Dorothy lingering nervously near the coat closet. She has brought two friends with her, maybe the only real friends who have entered her solitary life.

As I walk toward her I think fleetingly of all my adoptive relatives and my mother's and father's close friends who are attending the party. I pray silently that everyone will be compassionate and kind.

Dorothy squeezes me to her chest and leaves big red lipstick kisses on my cheeks, kisses so different from Marilyn's airy ones, intended to save our makeup from disaster.

Briefly, I sit with Dorothy, and we discuss matters of little importance. Our relationship, a mere two years young, is still strained. We are still trying to scale walls built over two-and-a-half decades.

One of the 151 other guests beckons me, and I tell Dorothy I will return later.

The wedding reception seems to have a life of its own. Everything that bridal magazines say about receptions is true. The day is a whirlwind. The newlyweds and their families do not eat the carefully selected food. They rarely dance to the carefully selected music. They never sit for long at any of the carefully selected table settings that feature carefully purchased decorations. And they never say more than a few words to each person they greet. There are just too many people vying for their attention.

By the time I am able to search out Dorothy again, nearly thirty minutes have gone by. I scan the room and see her friends, chatting nearby, but Dorothy is nowhere to be seen. Then suddenly I see my mother guiding Dorothy by the arm. She is introducing her to her family and friends, and I can tell by the look in her eyes that they had all better be warm and welcoming. My mother, though small in size, has a powerful personality. It is her best feature.

That moment, which was never captured by the photographer, will always remain in my memory. I have never witnessed a more touching scene. The courage and character of these two women is amazing.

I let them travel along together. I had decided prior to the party that I wouldn't introduce Dorothy to the guests as my mother. I struggled with exactly how to classify her, but on this day I felt that Marilyn deserved the title of mother at this party.

What I learn from these two women on this astonishing day is that it's OK to have two mothers.

What happens this afternoon is really like a miracle, except that it is accomplished not by magic, but by human love and acceptance.

These two have overcome their separate fears; my mother is able to thank Dorothy for giving her a child, and Dorothy is able to thank my mother for giving her child a home.

Most important, I am able to take the first step in accepting Dorothy as a mother in my life.

S.M. Eigenbrodt

Because I Promised

Dignity also comes from accepting and being confident in what you are.

My grandmother loved to talk of the farm where she was born and to reminisce about brothers and sisters and a favorite aunt who died in childbirth at the age of twenty-four. She talked lovingly of parents, later killed in the pogroms, whom she left forever at age sixteen, and her own longing for an education while growing up, an impossible dream for an impoverished girl.

Once, before preparing to light the Sabbath candles, she asked in a hushed tone if I would do her a favor.

"Anything, *Bubbie*" (Yiddish for grandmother).

"I would like to know how to write. Teach me to write my name."

She watched closely as I began to teach her. "Kate Goodman Sherman."

As much as my grandmother loved telling stories about her childhood, she loved to listen to my stories about school, friends, and just about anything else I chose to share. Whenever anything in my life troubled me and I would tell her about it, I would always feel better.

During such conversations, she would nod her head in rapt attention, drinking coffee or tea with a sugar cube in her mouth, sucking the coffee or tea through the cube. And she'd always explain that her way of drinking tea was not good manners—not something children lucky enough to be American-born should do.

There was another thing my grandmother insisted I not do. After finishing a rich cup of coffee, she would lift her saucer and drink the last drops that had fallen into it, enjoying herself immensely but insisting that it was a privilege of a different culture and not one I could share.

When I was young, she loved to rock me in her old comfortable rocking chair, the same one I have used for my two daughters. And when she was old and dying, she returned to this chair. I remember how she would nod her head in the twilight—looking so wise and beautiful—as we would sit together silently for hours.

Once I asked her if she would tell me the purpose of life—why we were here. "The purpose, darling, is your journey" is the only response she made to my question. But she answered another. "There will come a time when all pain is eased. Do not be afraid of life without me. My love will be yours forever."

On the last day that I spent with her, when death was very close, she said, in Yiddish of course, "I'd give anything for a saucer of my good coffee to drink, but promise me that you will never drink it that way." And she smiled bravely and reached for my hand. I tried to return her smile and promised as I clutched her hand. A few days later, she closed her eyes for the last time.

And now, in times of trouble or pain in my own life, I go into my kitchen, where her same containers for tea and coffee stand. And after brewing and enjoying some coffee, I look at the drops left in the saucer, remembering her words and feeling closer to her. I pick up the saucer, but I don't drink from it... because I promised.

And when my daughters are with me and see me remembering, I tell them what I know of their great-grandmother and the Lithuanian peasant village where she was raised. I tell them of her "old country" and her solitary journey to her new one and how good she was to me.

And I tell them that my love for her reaches beyond the stars.

Sara Kay Cohen

What you value is what you think about.
What you think about is what you become.
JOEL WELDON

In a Father's Heart

On a cold winter evening a man suffered a heart attack. After he was admitted into the hospital, he asked the nurse to call his daughter. He explained, "You see, I live alone and she is the only family I have." The nurse went and called the daughter.

The man's daughter on getting the news was quite upset and shouted, "You can't let him die! You see, Dad and I had a terrible argument almost a year ago. I haven't seen or spoken to him since. All these months I've wanted to go to him for forgiveness. The last thing I said to him was 'I hate you.'" The daughter cried and then said, "I'm coming now. I'll be there in thirty minutes."

The patient went into cardiac arrest, and his condition worsened even further. The nurse prayed, "O God, his daughter is coming. Please don't let it end this way. Let her get here before he dies." But the efforts of the medical team to revive the patient were fruitless.

After the man's daughter arrived, she learned the sad news. The nurse then observed one of the doctors talking to the daughter outside the room. She could see the pathetic hurt in her face. The nurse took the daughter aside and said, "I'm sorry for your terrible loss."

The daughter responded, "I never hated him, you know. I really loved him all the while. Please let me go to see him." The nurse escorted her to his room. The daughter went to the bed and buried her face and her countless tears in the sheets as she said good-bye to her deceased father.

The nurse tried not to look at this sad good-bye. But she

could not help but notice a scrap of paper on the bed table. The nurse picked up the paper and read it: "My dearest Barbara, I forgive you. I pray you will also forgive me. I know that you love me. I love you, too. Daddy."

Author Unknown

We pardon in the degree that we love.
FRANCOIS DE LA ROUCHEFOUCAULD

Between a Father and a Son

Aletter written during a war by a father to his soldier son:

Dear Son,
    I wish I had the power to write
    The thoughts wedged in my heart tonight
    As I sit watching that small star
    And wondering where and how you are.
    You know, Son, it's a funny thing
    How close a war can really bring
    A father, who for years with pride,
    Has kept emotions deep inside.
    I'm sorry, Son, when you were small
    I let reserve build up that wall;
    I told you real men never cried,
    And it was Mom who always dried
    Your tears and smoothed your hurts away
    So that you soon went back to play.
    But, Son, deep down within my heart
    I longed to have some little part
    In drying that small tear-stained face,
    But we were men—men don't embrace.
    And suddenly I found my son
    A full-grown man, with childhood done.
    Tonight you're far across the sea,
    Fighting a war for men like me.
    Well, somehow pride and what is right
    Have changed places here tonight

I find my eyes won't stay quite dry
And that men sometimes really cry.
And if we stood here, face to face,
I'm sure, my Son, we would embrace.

Author Unknown

---

*Nothing in life is to be feared.
It is only to be understood.*
MARIE CURIE

Love: A Variation on a Theme

If I live in a house of spotless beauty with everything in its place, but have not love, I am a housekeeper—not a homemaker.

If I have time for waxing, polishing, and decorative achievements, but have not love, my children learn cleanliness—not godliness.

Love leaves the dust in search of a child's laugh.

Love smiles at the tiny fingerprints on a newly cleaned window.

Love wipes away the tears before it wipes up the spilled milk.

Love picks up the child before it picks up the toys.

Love is present through the trials.

Love reprimands, reproves, and is responsive.

Love crawls with the baby, walks with the toddler, runs with the child, then stands aside to let the youth walk into adulthood.

Love is the key that opens salvation's message to a child's heart.

Before I became a mother I took glory in my house of perfection. Now I glory in God's perfection of my child.

As a mother there is much I must teach my child, but the greatest of all is love.

Jo Ann Merrill

Atmospheric Pressure

I don't feel well when I have to say, "I'm sorry." I get strong, flu-like symptoms. I become nauseated. My knees get weak, my hands shake, and I get facial ticks.

If I have to say, "I'm sorry and I was wrong," it's much worse. Then, along with the jerky behavior, my vision blurs, and my speech patterns slur.

I have noticed, though, that once I've said what needs to be said I make an amazing recovery.

One day, my husband Les was feeling frustrated with our eldest son over a work situation and needed to release a flurry of words. He came into my home office and spewed his displeasure about Marty onto me. Once Les said how he felt, he was ready to move past his aggravation.

After he left, I began to process their conflict and decided I could make the whole thing better. I envisioned myself as a Goodwill Angel (not to be confused with the Goodyear Blimp).

I fluttered into Marty's room and announced what he needed to do and when he needed to do it. For some reason Marty was not impressed with this angelic visitation.

In fact, he told me, "If Dad has a problem with me that's job-related, then he can talk to me."

Well, Marty might be twenty-five years old, but how dare he insinuate I was butting in? Setting aside my helping halo, in my loudest mother's voice I trumpeted my heated annoyance. I finally ended my tirade by stomping up the steps. Marty placed his exclamation point on our meeting by slamming out of the house.

I packed away my singed raiment and was still sizzling when I heard Les come in. I went down to make a pronouncement on his son's poor behavior. By the look on Les's face it was obvious he had already encountered Marty.

"If I wanted you to go to Marty, I would have asked you," he stated through clenched teeth. "Patsy, this was none of your business."

"None of my business!" I bellowed. A cloudburst of tears followed as I ran to my room, tripping several times on my lopsided wings.

"I was only trying to help," I kept consoling myself.

When the tears and the excuses stopped, I began to wonder if maybe I could have been wrong. Flu-like symptoms intensified when I realized I needed to apologize to both of them for interfering.

By the time I made my way out to Les and Marty, my vision had blurred. My head was pounding (probably from the heavy halo) as I stammered the dreaded words, "I-I was wr-wrong for interfering, I'm s-sorry, will you f-forgive me?"

Within moments we were all hugging.

As I walked back to the house, I noticed my headache and vexed vision had vanished, and it was almost... as if my feet weren't touching the ground.

Hey, Angel Face, anyone in your sphere deserve an apology?

Patsy Clairmont

It's Only Stuff

On July 18, 1989, I received a frantic call from my sister: our parents' home was on fire. Fortunately, I learned, no one was home—Mother was at her sister's cabin and Father was "out and about." This meant, however, that no one was able to retrieve irreplaceable family mementos.

During the twenty-mile drive to my parents' house, tears rolled down my cheeks as I thought about the destruction of the only tangible evidence of my youth. Then I heard a voice: *"It's only stuff, you know."* It was not spoken out loud, but it was clear and distinct, and comforting.

When my mother arrived from her sister's cabin, we surrounded her and gently led her to the charred remains of her home. Though she knew she was returning to a disaster, seeing the remains of her home was still a shock.

Fortunately, the firefighters had arrived in time to save the room containing many of our photo albums. When mother saw the albums, she was grateful that she had reacted a few weeks earlier to an inexplicable urge to move them from one room, now completely destroyed, to the only room left untouched by the blaze.

But we had lost many sentimental items, such as our Christmas decorations. Mother had saved the homemade ornaments we children had made throughout grade school, and I had loved showing them to my own children each year.

Among the most treasured possessions were ten Christmas stockings, one for each of us, handmade by our now-deceased grandmother. Each stocking was among the first gifts she would give her newest grandchild. Because I was the oldest in my family and one of the oldest grandchildren, I had often stood next to her, mesmerized, as she carefully stitched each stocking by hand. She decorated them with felt shapes of trains, angels, and—my favorite—Christmas trees, which were covered with brightly covered ornaments.

One of my brothers was convinced, against all reason, that these special remembrances of Gram had survived the fiery blaze. He therefore sifted through mound after mound of ashes and burned out blobs. Finally he found them—in a box under what remained of the basement stairwell. In the box was another treasure, remarkably unscathed: our nativity set. The family rejoiced at this discovery and said a prayer of gratitude.

None of this, though, was a match for what occurred on September 15, my parents' wedding anniversary. After church, they went out to the homesite for a last look at the remains of their home. By now, it had been bulldozed, and a crew was coming soon to clear away the last traces of the building.

As my parents approached the site, which was still wet from a heavy rain the night before, both spotted something white on the sidewalk. My mother gasped as she bent to pick up the object. It was the prayer book she had carried down the aisle thirty-eight years ago, to the day. And it was bone-dry. My father says an angel placed it there.

The fire had destroyed pretty much of all the other material possessions my parents had ever owned. But as we reflected on the significance of the items that did survive the fire, we realized each one was symbolic. The wedding prayer book, for example, is tangible proof of my parents' spirituality and religious beliefs, which we, their children, now try to pass on to our children. And every Christmas, as we hang those ten stockings, now lightly browned around the edges, we are reminded of the grandmother who made them. Finally, the photographs help us all recall our youth and remember the importance of family.

The love and happiness contained within the walls of the old house have expanded into ten more households. Those good feelings emerge often, whenever we gather as a clan that now numbers over fifty.

I can still hear my mother's voice calling me as a teenager as I would back out of the driveway, with a carful of my siblings, "Be careful, honey!" she'd say. "You have my most precious possessions in that car!"

We still are her most precious possessions. The rest, after all, is just "stuff."

Mary Treacy O'Keefe

Life is either a daring adventure or nothing . . .
Security is mostly a superstition. It does not exist in nature.
HELEN KELLER

Newfangled Inventions

~❤~

My Grandmother Melton loves answering machines. She'll call me up and say, "I can't find anybody home. And I thought to myself, 'I'll just call Joy' 'cause even if you're not there I can talk to you anyway." She'll use all the time, then call back and leave another message. She tells me all kinds of things. It's great.

One time she told me how she got the flu at Uncle Hambone's and "upchucked all over the house." Or she'll tell me about all the vegetables she's gotten out of the garden.

I'm always delighted when I come home to find one message light blinking or two, and I hit the rewind button and it takes forever. I know that Granny has called. They're verbal letters.

My other grandmother, whom I lost recently, was an interesting character, too. Even if she was wrong, she was right. For instance, Geraldo may pronounce his name *Heraldo*, but no, for Granny, it was *Geraldo*: "It says right there on the screen G-e-r-a-l-d-o."

When I gave her a Kodak instant camera, she used it to take pictures of every neighborhood stray or every flower she had growing in the yard. I guess that was her world, so she had piles and piles of pictures of the flowers and the dogs. The camera quit working once, and she said, "I don't know why it's not working. I spilt some milk inside but I wiped it out." When Kodak issued a recall on those cameras, that was the most exciting thing my grandmother had ever had happen and the most fun. You got to send it in and get money.

Joy Melton Prickett

It's Possible

The teacher asked her class what each wanted to become when they grew up. A chorus of responses came from all over the room. "A football player." "A doctor." "An astronaut." "The president." "A fireman." "A teacher." "A race car driver." Everyone in the classroom had a response. Everyone, that is, except Tommy. The teacher noticed he was sitting there quiet and still.

So she said to him, "Tommy, what do you want to be when you grow up?"

"Possible," Tommy replied.

"Possible?" asked the teacher.

"Yes," Tommy said, "my mom is always telling me I'm impossible. So when I get to be big, I want to become *possible*."

Author Unknown

---

*Life's under no obligation to give us what we expect.
We take what we get and are thankful it's no worse than it is.*
MARGARET MITCHELL

The Present

While a grown man was awaiting surgery in a hospital he began talking with his father. "I sure hope I can be home by Father's Day," he said. The two recalled various Father's Day celebrations they had shared through the years and then the son said wistfully, "I still feel awful that when I was ten years old, I didn't give you either a card or a gift."

The father replied, "Son, I remember the Saturday before that Father's Day. I saw you in a store, although you didn't see me. I watched as you picked up several cigars and stuffed them in your pocket. I knew you had no money, and I suspected you were about to steal those cigars as a present for me. I felt extremely sad to think you would leave the store without paying for them. But almost as soon as you tucked the cigars in your pocket, you pulled them out and put them back in the box on the shelf.

"When you stayed out playing all the next day because you had no present to give me, you probably thought I was hurt. You were wrong. When you put those cigars back and decided not to break the law, you gave me the best Father's Day present I ever received."

Author Unknown

Happiness is not the end of life; character is.
HENRY WARD BEECHER

Remembering Dad

A family on the East Coast was planning a month's vacation in California. At the last minute the father's work responsibilities prevented him from going with the family. Mom insisted that she was more than able to take charge of all the arrangements as well as the driving. It was decided that she and the kids would go ahead with the trip. Dad got out the maps and together they planned the route they would take and where the family should stop each night.

Within a couple of weeks after the family departed, the father was able to finish his extra work responsibilities. So he decided to surprise the family and join them on their trip. So he flew out to a city in California without telling them or calling them. Then he took a taxi out to the country highway that, according to his travel plan, his family should be driving down later that day. The taxi driver dropped him off on the side of the road and he stood there waiting. Within the hour he saw the family car coming. He stuck out his thumb as a hitchhiker would do.

Mom and the kids drove right past him. They couldn't believe their eyes. One of the children shouted out, "Hey, wasn't that Dad we just passed?" Mom screeched to a stop, backed up to the hitchhiker, and the family shared a joyful reunion.

Later, when a reporter from the local paper got wind of such an unusual story, he asked the man why he would do such a crazy thing. He responded, "After I die, I want my kids to be able to say, 'Dad sure was fun, wasn't he?'"

Author Unknown

Thoughts to Console Parents Whose Kids Have Moved Back In

~♥~

It's impossible to love the same child for twenty years. (After twenty years, it's not the same child.)

Grown-up kids are like winter storms. They may be late, but they never fail to show up.

Consider yourself a successful parent if they flip off the headlights before turning into the driveway at four in the morning.

Remember when you worried because you didn't know where your children were? Now, you do. They're back in their own rooms.

When children return to the family home, it's a gesture of reciprocal love. You drove them to school and now they're driving you up the wall.

You can't reason with them, and you can't hit them. How did they get so big and strong on junk food?

Why did they have to return just when everything started to click for you? (Your teeth, your knees, your back.)

It isn't aimed at you, personally. When newlyweds can't scratch up enough chicken feed to feather their own nest, they come home and pluck their parents.

You never realize what a happy marriage you've had until the kids move back—and then it's too late.

Before they left, the kids were deductible. Now, they're just taxing.

Author Unknown

No matter how old a mother is she watches her middle-aged children for signs of improvement.
FLORIDA SCOTT-MAXWELL

The Ears That Know

A little girl shouted with glee at the unexpected appearance of her grandmother in her nursery. "I've come to tuck you into bed and give you a goodnight kiss," the grandmother explained.

"Will you read me a story first?" the little girl asked. Grandma, dressed elegantly for the impending dinner party downstairs, couldn't resist the soulful plea in her granddaughter's eyes.

"All right," she replied, "but just one."

At the close of the story, the little girl snuggled into her bed, ready for sleep, but not before she said, "Thank you, Grandma. You look pretty tonight."

The grandmother smiled and replied, "Yes, I have to be pretty for the dinner party your parents are hosting."

"I know," the little girl said. "Mommy and Daddy are entertaining some very important people downstairs."

"Why, yes," said the grandmother. "But how did you know that? Was it because I surprised you by coming upstairs tonight? Was it my dress that gave it away?" Each time her granddaughter shook her head with a vigorous "no." Finally, the grandmother asked, "Was it that I only read *one* story to you?"

"No," the little girl giggled. "Just listen! Mommy is laughing at all of Daddy's jokes."

Author Unknown

What It's Worth

Two young toughs stood at a certain corner in Brooklyn, hiding themselves behind the edge of a building, waiting for a certain man. They had watched this man pass the corner at precisely 6:30 each evening, laden with grocery bags and a lunch pail. They had also spied the outline of a fat wallet in his hip pocket behind his short jacket.

It seemed obvious to them that he brought his pay home each day in cash—cash they eagerly anticipated would be theirs with only a few clever moves and the element of surprise on their side.

Promptly at 6:30 the man appeared, striding with a purpose born of having somewhere meaningful to go. The boys tensed and then sprang from their hiding place. The attack was over in an instant.

Before he really knew what had hit him, the man was lying on the ground, his head swimming, groceries scattered around him. The thugs raced two blocks away down an alley. "Whew! Man!" they laughed. "Let's see how much we got!"

Four hands scrambled to open the bulging wallet. Their eyes grew wide as they surveyed the contents—two dollars and two long foldouts of picture after picture of the man's six children.

Author Unknown

FIVE

LOVE ADDS a LITTLE CHOCOLATE... TO LEARNING

---

*The Golden Rule is of no use whatsoever
unless you realize
that it is YOUR move.*
DR. FRANK CRANE

CALVIN AND HOBBES

Learning from Our Decisions

The young man was only thirty-two when he was appointed president of the bank. He'd never dreamed he'd ever become president, much less at such a young age. One day he was speaking with the chairman of the board whom he had replaced as president. "You know, I've just been appointed president and it is an awesome job. With your many years of experience, I was wondering if you could give me some sound advice."

The old man looked at the new president seated before him and immediately came back with just two words: "Right decisions!"

The young man had hoped for a bit more than this, so he said, "That's really helpful, and I appreciate it. But can you be more specific? I really need your help so that I make right decisions."

The wise old man, being a person of few words, simply responded, "Experience."

The new bank president said, "Well, that's just the point of my being here. I don't have the kind of experience I need. How do I get it?"

The old man smiled and tersely replied, "Wrong decisions!"

Author Unknown

You cannot create experience, you undergo it.
ALBERT CAMUS

A Brush with Death—and Life

A couple of weeks ago, my children and I were almost killed crossing the street right in front of our apartment building. I was walking them to their last day of school. Three-quarters of the way across, with the light in our favor and all of us dutifully holding hands, a car burst out of nowhere, hurtling around the corner at breakneck speed, ricocheting off the curb, and swerving into our path.

I saw the driver clearly. We were so close we could have kissed. She was a beautiful woman with wild eyes. Missing us by inches, her car skidded, fishtailed back into control, and disappeared. I could barely breathe, my knees buckling, my heart beating like a pile driver. In stark contrast, my kids just laughed, romping blithely down the sidewalk, jumping from tree to tree as they always do, trying to touch the leaves.

Deeply shaken, not knowing what to think or say, I did the obvious thing. I got angry. Not at the driver, of course. She was gone. I vented my anger at the children. I decided to teach them a lesson they obviously had failed to learn from the experience.

"Never, never let your guard down when you're crossing the street. Did you see that car? It almost hit us. It really did. We could have been killed."

"Come off it, Dad," my eight-year-old son replied nonchalantly, jumping a second time at a branch that had eluded him. By this time my six-year-old daughter was skipping around the next corner and was almost out of sight.

That did it. I exploded. If they remember anything about our somber walk to school that morning, it is that their father sometimes, with the slightest provocation, lapses into fits of wild irrationality. And they were right. Neither of them was doing anything wrong. They were holding my hands, walking with the signal. I had no lesson to teach them.

Only this, perhaps: Our lives are beset with trapdoors. Whenever the ground seems most secure, someone out there has his hand on the lever. A massive coronary, an embolism, a drunk driver, a strung-out addict drawing a pound of flesh for an ounce of crack. When the trapdoor springs, we haven't time for regrets or second chances, for anger or recrimination. It just happens. Swoosh. No good-byes.

I try to teach my children about life's dangers. We all do. Look both ways. Wear white after dark. Don't take candy from strangers. We answer their questions and dearly wish they'd ask us more. But put a mad driver behind the wheel and our lessons mean nothing.

Trapdoors have one saving grace: They add to our appreciation for life, even as they threaten to extinguish it. That very afternoon, as I walked my son and daughter home from school, they looked different to me, more vulnerable and precious. As we talked about their day at school and our summer plans, I loved them desperately.

It reminded me of something that I keep forgetting: Life is not a given, but a priceless gift. One day something will steal it from us, a seizure in the night or a driver in the morning, but that doesn't diminish its value. On the contrary, fragility and impermanence ensure life's preciousness. We can truly love only that which one day we must lose. It took a trap-door trembling beneath my feet, and a crazed woman casting the shadow of death across my family's path, to awaken me once again to the wonder of life and the blessings of love.

But that's the way it is. Often, the most precious gifts come wrapped in odd packages. So odd, in fact, that if given a choice, almost certainly we would choose the wrong one. The one in fancy paper and topped with a bow. Never the one in brown paper wrapping tied with a string.

They didn't know it, but my kids had the right idea. We had just escaped from a brush with death. Why didn't I think to jump and touch the leaves?

E. Forrester Church

The way to love anything is to realize that it might be lost.
G.K. CHESTERTON

A Lesson for Life

"Look at fatso!" Freshmen in high school can be cruel, and we certainly were to a young man named Matt who was in my class. We mimicked him, teased him, and taunted him about his size. He was at least fifty pounds overweight. He felt the pain of being the last one picked to play basketball, baseball, or football. Matt will always remember the endless pranks that were played on him—trashing his hall locker, piling library books on his desk at lunch time, and spraying him with icy streams of water in the shower after gym class.

One day he sat near me in gym class. Someone pushed him and he fell on me and banged my foot quite badly. The kid who pushed him said Matt did it. With the whole class watching I was put on the spot to either shrug it off or pick a fight with Matt. I chose to fight in order to keep my image intact.

I shouted, "C'mon, Matt, let's fight." He said he didn't want to. But peer pressure forced him into the conflict whether he liked it or not. He came toward me with his fists in the air. He was no George Foreman. With one punch I bloodied his nose and the class went wild. Just then the gym teacher walked into the room. He saw that we were fighting and he sent us out to the oval running track.

But then he said something that left a lasting impression. He declared with a smile, "I want you two guys to go out there and run that mile holding each other's hands." The room erupted into a roar of laughter. The two of us were embarrassed beyond belief, but Matt and I went out to the track and ran our mile—hand in hand.

At some point during the course of our run, I remember looking over at him, with blood still trickling from his nose and his weight slowing him down. It struck me that here was a person, not all that different than myself. We both looked at each other and began to laugh. In time we became good friends. For the rest of my life I have never so much as raised a hand against another person.

Going around that track, hand in hand, I no longer saw Matt as fat or dumb. He was a human being who had intrinsic value and worth far beyond any externals. It was amazing what I learned when I was forced to go hand-in-hand with someone for only a mile.

Medard Laz

———

The turning point in the process of growing up is when you discover the core strength within you that survives all hurt.
MAX LERNER

———

A Father's Wish

I write this... as a father. Until you have a son of your own, you will never know what that means. You will never know the joy beyond joy, the love beyond feeling that resonates in the heart of a father as he looks upon his son. You will never know the sense of honor that makes a man want to be more than he is and to pass on something good and hopeful into the hands of his son. And you will never know the heart-break of the fathers who are haunted by the personal demons that keep them from being the men they want their sons to see.

You will only see the man that stands before you, or who ıas left your life, who exerts a power over you—for good or for ill—that will never let go.

It is a great privilege and a great burden to be that man. There is something that must be passed from father to son, or it is never passed as clearly. It is a sense of manhood, of self-worth, of responsibility to the world around us.

And yet, how to put it in words? We live in a time when it is hard to speak from the heart. Our lives are smothered by a thousand trivialities and the poetry of our spirits is silenced by the thoughts and cares of daily affairs. The song that lives in our hearts, the song that we have waited to share, the song of being a man, is silent. We find ourselves full of advice but devoid of belief.

And so, I want to speak to you honestly. I do not have answers. But I do understand the questions. I see you struggling and discovering and striving upward, and I see myself reflected in your eyes and in your days. In some deep and fundamental way, I have been there, and I want to share.

I, too, have learned to walk, to run, to fall. I have had a first love. I have known fear and anger and sadness. My heart has been broken and I have known moments when the hand of God seemed to be on my shoulder. I have wept tears of sorrow and tears of joy.

There have been times of darkness when I thought I would never again see light, and there have been times when I wanted to dance and sing and hug every person I met.

I have felt myself emptied into the mystery of the universe, and I have had moments when the smallest slight threw me into a rage.

I have carried others when I barely had the strength to walk myself, and I have left others standing by the side of the road with their hands outstretched for help.

Sometimes I feel I have done more than anyone can ask; other times I feel I am a charlatan and a failure. I carry within me the spark of greatness and the darkness of heartless crimes.

In short, I am a man, as are you.

Although you will walk your own earth and move through your own time, the same sun will rise on you that rose on me, and the same seasons will course across your life as moved across mine. We will always be different, but we will always be the same.

This is my attempt to give you the lessons of my life, so that you can use them in yours. They are not meant to make you into me. It is my greatest joy to watch you become yourself. But time reveals truths, and these truths are greater than either of us. If I can give them a voice in a way that allows me to walk beside you during your days, then I will have done well.

To be your father is the greatest honor I have ever received. It allowed me to touch mystery for a moment, and to see my love made flesh. If I could have but one wish, it would be for you to pass that love along. After all, there is not much more to life than that.

Kent Nerburn

It's a wonderful feeling when your father becomes not a god but a man to you–when he comes down from the mountain and you see he's this man with weaknesses. And you love him as this whole being, not as a figurehead.
ROBIN WILLIAMS

My Dad Loved My Mom

I didn't learn about love from a new boy in town or a bronzed lifeguard, but from a fortyish father of eight: my dad.

The summer I was thirteen, our family moved from the East Coast to Arizona. Mom flew ahead with the baby to Tucson. The rest of us piled into the station wagon for the long cross-country drive. After four days of turnpikes and highways, we arrived, punchy and tired—in Sioux City, Iowa, my mother's hometown.

We were ready for a break. Visiting and playing with our cousins for a couple of days was just what we needed. On the last afternoon of our stay, Dad took me aside. "Let's go for a ride," he said. "Just you and me." He didn't have to ask twice.

Every landmark absorbed his attention. We drove slowly past the buildings of downtown Sioux City. We passed the famous stockyards and headed north to the suburb of Leeds. Dad seemed to know where he was going as we wound through the quiet, residential streets.

We pulled up to a rambling, two-story yellow house and he switched off the motor. Like all the homes in the neighborhood, this one was set back from a wide, tree-lined avenue.

"The house used to be gray back then," Dad said, peering through the windshield.

"Back when?"

"A long time ago. That's the house your mother lived in when I first met her," he mused. "I sent a lot of letters to 610 Eighteenth Street."

We stepped out of the car and stood for a moment. *My mother really lived there?* I remembered a story Mom told me about her father planting a vegetable garden during World War II; even the front yard had to be sacrificed. No signs of a garden existed now.

Dad motioned to me, and we began to walk. Both of us were lost in thought.

"Was this street the same when you met Mom?" I asked.

"Pretty much," replied Dad. "Only it was spring. You know how budding trees are a kind of bright green that only lasts for a couple of weeks? Well, that's how it was back then—everywhere. I remember lots of tulips and big bushes full of white flowers."

"Why were you here, Daddy?"

"I was stationed out at Sgt. Bluff Army-Air Force Base. That's before I joined the paratroopers and went to Europe. I'd take the bus into town and get off back there on Fourth Street. I used to run all the way. I never got winded."

I remembered a picture of Dad in his army uniform—khaki trousers tucked into shiny black boots, a jaunty look on his youthful face.

We spent a few more minutes gazing at the yellow house. "Your mom and I used to go for a treat a couple of blocks away," said Dad. "If it's still there, I'll buy you an ice cream."

We made a game of stepping over the sidewalk cracks. Roots from the giant elms thrust the concrete upward, forming an obstacle course. The summer sun flickered through the shade of our leafy canopy.

"It's still there," he said triumphantly. And so we crossed the street to a large Victorian building facing the intersection. Gallantly Dad opened the arched door. We laughed as my "date" waltzed me into the Green Gables Ice Cream Emporium.

In a booth by the window, I pondered the delicious dilemma of flavors. "What kind did Mom get?" I asked. He thought for a minute: "Usually chocolate chip."

"Then I'll get a chocolate chip, too," I said. He grinned like the paratrooper in the picture.

"And I'll order my old favorite: pistachio." He set the menu aside with a flourish.

Dad's stories flowed freely while we savored our ice cream. It seems Mom wore a red dress on their first date—Easter Sunday, 1943. He had just turned nineteen, and Mom invited him to meet her folks.

Dad told me about concerts in Grandview Park, and the time Mom got off work to wave good-bye at the train depot the day he shipped out to Fort Benning, Georgia. When Dad won a three-day pass, he used it to ride the rails all the way back to Iowa. Of course, he was late getting back to the fort and had KP duty for weeks.

I listened transfixed. My thirteen-year-old imagination recreated every scene. As he spun his tales, his face took on a faraway look.

He really misses Mom. The thought was a surprise to my adolescent understanding of parents. It touched me that he could remember every detail of their courtship and share it with me. For the first time in my young life, I saw that Dad loved Mom in a deep, emotional way. And he not only loved her, he was *in love* with her. He brightened just at the thought of her.

After fifteen years of marriage, Mom remained the young woman he met in a Midwestern town and fell in love with.

In that moment, a father gave his thirteen-year-old daughter a priceless gift. I glimpsed how real and romantic married love can be; and I knew I'd never settle for less. On the threshold of my own teen years, I learned a beautiful truth as the years melted away and a young soldier asked me out to the Green Gables for ice cream.

Kathleen MacInnis Kichline

There's a time when you have to explain to your children why they're born, and it's a marvelous thing if you know the reason by then.
HAZEL SCOTT

I Can... and I Cannot

I *gave you life*
   but I cannot live it for you.
I can teach you things
   but I cannot make you learn.
I can give you directions
   but I cannot always be there to lead you.
I can allow you freedom
   but I cannot account for it.
I can take you to church
   but I cannot make you believe.
I can teach you right from wrong
   but I cannot always decide for you.
I can buy you beautiful clothes
   but I cannot make you lovely inside.
I can offer you advice
   but I cannot accept it for you.
I can give you love
   but I cannot force it upon you.

I can teach you to be a friend
   but I cannot make you one.
I can teach you to share
   but I cannot make you unselfish.
I can teach you respect
   but I can't force you to show honor.
I can grieve about your report card
   but I cannot doubt your teachers.

I can advise you about friends
  but I cannot choose them for you.
I can teach you about sex
  but I cannot keep you pure.
I can tell you the facts of life
  but I can't build your reputation.
I can tell you about drink
  but I can't say NO for you.
I can warn you about drugs
  but I can't prevent you from using them.
I can tell you about lofty goals
  but I can't achieve them for you.
I can let you baby-sit
  but I can't be responsible for your actions.

I can teach you kindness
  but I can't force you to be gracious.
I can warn you about sins
  but I cannot make your morals.
I can love you as a child
  but I cannot place you in God's family.
I can pray for you
  but I cannot make you walk with God.

Author Unknown

A Real Shine

It seems as though
    there is never enough time
        to do all the things
            we have to do.
Or is there?
When I got to work today,
    I realized
        that my shoes weren't shined.
I bent over to shine them at home this morning,
    but heard my little son crying
        before I got the lid off the polish.
So I went to him
    and picked him up
        and dried his tears
            and gave him love.
Then I didn't have time
    to go back and shine my shoes.
I had to leave.
That's OK.
Some day my shoes will be in a scrap heap
    and no one will care
        whether they were ever shined.
But the love I gave my son this morning
    will live on in him
        and those he passes it on to.
No, I'm not embarrassed
    that my shoes aren't shined.
They're a sign that I'm learning
    to keep first things first.

John Gile

Criticism or Encouragement?

I was twelve years old. Because my father's work moved from the north of England to the south, I had to change schools in midyear. In my new school people talked differently, and my accent was wrong. As I was very sensitive, it is not surprising that I felt unaccepted, lonely, and unhappy.

One morning, the vice-principal, who used to "prowl" around the classes, stood behind me as I tried to write up my first science experiment. Fixing her eyes on my page, in a loud voice she said to the teacher, "Miss T___, would you tell me what 'sluphic acid' is?" I'd never before seen or even heard of its being spelled "sulphuric" acid. (Today I'm amused that my American dictionary says, "This spelling is no longer admitted by scientific publications.")

Another teacher gave me my introduction to geometry. After a difficult lesson on a particularly intricate diagram, she said to me, "You ought to become an architect; you take such great care over every detail."

I have never forgotten those two experiences, and there is no doubt which of the two has had the greater influence upon my life. Through the years I have learned, too, that encouragement is not only a sound method of teaching children; it is also a way of cultivating relationships in all of life.

Vera Chapman Mace

Praise, like gold or diamonds, owes its value to its scarcity.
SAMUEL JOHNSON

Growing Up

When I was growing up I didn't like my dad very much. My parents were divorced, and I grew up with my mother who really colored my views of him. He knew that I didn't like him and didn't want to spend time with him.

Dad had a summer house in New Hampshire about an hour's drive from where I grew up. It's a lake house in the town where he grew up. He wanted me to love it, but I didn't want to go there and remember telling him that I didn't want to see him. We went anyway, and, boy, was it awkward. I was about ten.

Now I love to go to the lake house. The water is so pure it's amazing. I always skinny-dip and it feels so good, like silk.

My dad and my Uncle Jed made a totem pole there one year. They cut down the tree and everything and it took a long time. There are three different carvings: one has wings, one had a real long nose, and one has freckles on it. When I was growing up, I had tons of freckles, and they put the freckles on there for me.

Dave DeGrandpre

Children need love, especially when they don't deserve it.
HAROLD S. HULBERT

Our Uniqueness

One wise teacher was speaking to a group of eager young students. He gave them the assignment to go out and find a small, unnoticed flower somewhere. He asked them to study the flower for a long time. "Get a magnifying glass and study the delicate veins in the leaves, and notice the nuances and shades of color. Turn the leaves slowly and observe their symmetry. And remember that this flower might have gone unnoticed and unappreciated if you had not found and admired it."

After the class returned, the teacher observed, "People are like that. Each one is different, carefully crafted, uniquely endowed. But you have to spend time with them to know this. So many people go unnoticed and unappreciated because no one has ever taken time with them and admired their uniqueness."

John Powell

Every person is an exception.
SÖREN KIERKEGAARD

If I Had My Life to Live Over

If I had my life to live over, I would have talked less and listened more.

Instead of wishing away nine months of pregnancy and complaining about the shadow over my feet, I'd have cherished every minute of it, and realized that the baby growing inside me was my only chance to assist God in the miracle.

I would have invited friends over for dinner even if the carpet was stained and the sofa faded.

I would have eaten popcorn in the "good" living room and worried less about the dirt when you lit the fireplace.

I would have taken time to listen to my grandfather ramble about his youth.

I would have sat cross-legged on the lawn with my children and never worried about grass stains.

I would have cried and laughed less while watching TV... and more while watching real life.

I would have gone to bed when I was sick instead of pretending the earth would go into a holding pattern if I weren't there for a day.

I would never have bought anything just because it was practical, wouldn't show dirt, or was guaranteed to last a lifetime.

When my child kissed me impetuously, I would never have said, "Later. Now go get washed up for dinner."

There would have been more I-love-you's, more I'm-listening's. But mostly, given another shot at life, I would seize every minute of it. Look at it and really see it. Try it on, live it, exhaust it, and never give that minute back until there was nothing left of it.

Author Unknown

Out of the Mouths...

The teacher was making out a registration card. "What is your father's name?" she asked.

"Daddy," answered the little girl.

"Yes, I know. But what does your mother call him?"

"Mother doesn't call him anything," the little girl replied. "She likes him."

Author Unknown

Every child comes with the message that God is not yet discouraged of man.
RABINDRANATH TAGORE

Ten Commandments for Parents

1. My hands are small. Please don't expect perfection whenever I make a bed, draw a picture, or throw a ball. My legs are short. Slow down so that I can keep up with you.

2. My eyes have not seen the world as yours have. Let me explore it safely. Don't restrict me unnecessarily.

3. Housework will always be there. I'm little only for a short time. Take time to explain things to me about this wonderful world, and do so willingly.

4. My feelings are tender. Don't nag me all day long (you would not want to be nagged for your inquisitiveness). Treat me as you would like to be treated.

5. I am a special gift from God. Treasure me as God intended you to do—holding me accountable for my actions, giving me guidelines to live by, and disciplining me in a loving manner.

6. I need your encouragement (but not your empty praise) to grow. Go easy on the criticism. Remember, you can criticize the things I do without criticizing me.

7. Give me the freedom to make decisions concerning myself. Permit me to fail, so that I can learn from my mistakes. Then someday I'll be prepared to make the decisions life will require of me.

8. Don't do things over for me. That makes me feel that my efforts didn't measure up to your expectations. I know it's hard, but don't compare me with my brother or my sister.

9. Don't be afraid to leave for a weekend together. Kids need vacations from parents, and parents need vacations from kids. Besides, it's a great way to show us kids your marriage is something special.

10. Take me to Sunday school and church regularly, setting a good example for me to follow. I enjoy learning more about God.

Kevin Leman

Blessed be childhood, which brings down something of heaven into the midst of our rough earthiness.
HENRI FREDERIC AMIEL

SIX

LOVE ADDS a LITTLE CHOCOLATE... TO ACHIEVING

---

*Success has nothing to do with
what you gain in life or accomplish for yourself.
Success is what you do for others.*
DANNY THOMAS

PEANUTS reprinted by permission of United Features Syndicate, Inc.

Overcoming Obstacles

~❤~

Some of the world's most renowned women and men have had to overcome disabilities and adversities that would have crushed a more fragile soul. Like butterflies breaking out of cocoons, these great historical figures struggled against—and rose above—the confines of circumstance in a way that makes their achievements even more remarkable. While hardship alone does not produce genius, some might argue that the "recipe" for true greatness includes a liberal dash of resilience....

Sometimes the source of the difficulty is medical. A child born to a woman dying of tuberculosis became Marie Curie. Infantile paralysis did not hold back Franklin D. Roosevelt. And even the loss of his hearing could not diminish the great composer Ludwig van Beethoven.

Social and economic barriers are also real but not insurmountable. A child raised in abject poverty could become another Abraham Lincoln or Enrico Caruso. Being born black in a society filled with racial discrimination did not stop Booker T. Washington, Martin Luther King, Harriet Tubman, Marian Anderson, Jesse Owens, or George Washington Carver from realizing their potential.

Educational barriers will not stop the truly gifted. Think of Albert Einstein. This genius was called a "slow learner," "retarded," and "uneducable." And yet he lived to disprove them all.

Finally, multiple hindrances are not enough to hamper true greatness. A Jewish child, born of Nazi concentration camp survivors and paralyzed from the waist down at the age of four, grew to become the incomparable concert violinist Itzhak Perlman.

Author Unknown

The Greatest Moment

A reporter once interviewed the famous contralto Marian Anderson and asked her to name the greatest moment of her life. The reporter knew she had many big moments from which to choose.

He expected her to name the private concert she gave at the White House for the Roosevelts and the King and Queen of England. He thought that she might name the night she received the $10,000 Bok Award as the person who had done the most for her home town, Philadelphia.

Instead, Marian Anderson shocked him by responding quickly, "The greatest moment of my life was the day I went home and told my mother she wouldn't have to take in washing anymore."

The circular pattern of love between parent and child is more than a matter of "what goes around, comes around." Rather, it stems from the principle that what a child sees, a child copies. Children are not born to be selfless and generous. Their more common cries are rooted in "Me first! Mine! I want it!"

A child must learn to share, to sacrifice for others, to give spontaneously and from the heart. And a child learns that lesson most easily by copying someone else—usually his mother or father.

Author Unknown

The Sunshine

There was an old violinist who was poor, but he owned an instrument that never failed to charm his listeners with its soothing mellowness. Played as only he could play it, it never failed to awaken responsive chords in the heart.

Asked to explain its charm, he would hold out his violin and, tenderly caressing its graceful curves, say: "Ah, a great deal of sunshine must have gone into this wood, and what has gone in comes out!"

E. Townley Lord

Those who bring sunshine into the lives of others
cannot keep it from themselves.
Sir James Barrie

Tigers in the Dark

Several years ago there was a well-known television circus show that developed a Bengal tiger act. Like the rest of the show, it was done "live" before a large audience. One evening, the tiger trainer went into the cage with several tigers to do a routine performance. The door was locked behind him. The spotlights highlighted the cage, the television cameras moved in close, and the audience watched in suspense as the trainer skillfully put the tigers through their paces.

In the middle of the performance, the worst possible fate befell the act: the lights went out! For twenty or thirty long, dark seconds the trainer was locked in with the tigers. In the darkness they could see him, but he could not see them. A whip and a small kitchen chair seemed meager protection under the circumstances, but he survived, and when the lights came on, he calmly finished the performance.

In an interview afterward, he was asked how he felt knowing that the tigers could see him but that he could not see them. He first admitted the chilling fear of the situation, but pointed out that the tigers did not know that he could not see them. He said, "I just kept cracking my whip and talking to them until the lights came on. And they never knew I could not see them as well as they could see me."

This experience gives us a vivid parable of human life. At some point in our lives, all of us face the terrifying task of fighting tigers in the dark.

Thomas Lane Butts

Built on Solid Rock

There were four children born a year apart in the family and they had outgrown the house they were living in. Henry, the father, didn't earn very much money as a police reporter for a newspaper. But one afternoon, his wife Jane picked up her children at school and said, "I'm going to build us a house."

Her children chimed in, "What do you know about building a house?" She replied, "I'm going to learn."

So Jane went and talked to the brick mason and the electrician and the plumber. She learned how to build a house. She dug the foundation with her own hands with a pick and shovel, she laid the blocks, she put in the wiring, she put in the plumbing, and Henry would help her with some of the heavy work when he got home from work. She built her home and her family with her own two hands using sheer determination.

As her daughter Janet remembers her, Jane lavished on her children the kind of love that empowered, not enslaved. She taught all four of her children how to play baseball, bake a cake, and play fair.

As Janet recalls, "She beat the living daylights out of us sometimes, and she loved us with all her heart. She taught us her favorite poets. And there is no child care in the world that will ever be a substitute for what that lady was in our lives. My mother always told me to do my best, to think my best, and to do right and consider myself a person."

Another daughter, Maggy, recalls, "What gave us our self-confidence was the absolute certainty that every adult in our world loved us absolutely. They weren't always perfect, and we weren't always perfect. But we could count on that love."

Jane received love in return. Her daughter Janet declined to be considered for a job in President Clinton's administration until after her mother's death so she might remain by her ailing mother's side.

When Janet Reno finally did accept a position, it was as Attorney General of the United States, the first woman to head the Justice Department of our country.

When not in Washington, Janet Reno still lives in the house that her mother built in south Florida. She remarks: "I have lived in that house ever since, and as I come down the driveway through the woods at night, with a problem, with an obstacle to overcome, that house is a symbol to me that you can do anything you really want if it's the right thing to do and you put your mind to it."

Author Unknown

People often say that this or that person
has not yet found himself.
But self is not something that one finds.
It is something that one creates.
THOMAS SZASZ

The Best News of All

When Eleanor Sass was a child, she was hospitalized for appendicitis. Her roommate was a young girl named Mollie, who was injured when an automobile hit the bicycle she was riding. Mollie's legs had been badly broken and though the doctors performed several surgeries, Mollie faced a strong possibility that she would never walk again.

She became depressed, uncooperative, and cried a great deal. She only seemed to perk up when the morning mail arrived. Most of her gifts were books, games, stuffed animals—all appropriate gifts for a bedridden child.

Then one day a different sort of gift came, this one from an aunt far away. When Mollie tore open the package, she found a pair of shiny, black-patent-leather shoes. The nurses in the room mumbled something about "people who don't use their heads," but Mollie didn't seem to hear them. She was too busy putting her hands in the shoes and "walking" them up and down her blanket.

From that day, her attitude changed. She began cooperating with the nursing staff, and soon she was in therapy. One day Eleanor heard that her friend had left the hospital, and the best news of all, she had walked out, wearing her shiny new shoes.

Author Unknown

What oxygen is to the lungs, such is hope to the meaning of life.
EMIL BRUNNER

Facing the World

A young man began his studies at a well-known college and was on crutches everywhere he went on campus. He was a friendly, gregarious, and optimistic person and soon he had the respect and friendship of many of his classmates.

One day a fellow student asked him what had caused his deformity that necessitated his crutches. "Infantile paralysis," he replied. His succinct answer sent the message that he did not want to get into any details about his situation.

But his classmate wanted further insight. So he inquired, "With a misfortune like that, how can you face the world so cheerfully?"

"Oh," he responded with a smile, "the disease never touched my heart."

Author Unknown

---

*You gain strength, courage, and confidence by every
experience in which you really stop to look fear in the face.
You are able to say to yourself, "I lived through this horror.
I can take the next thing that comes along."*
ELEANOR ROOSEVELT

The Woman Who Wouldn't Pray

The chaplain had tried everything with the woman but prayer—her prayer. Oh, he had prayed, ever since the doctors admitted there was nothing they could do but keep her comfortable. But she was so bitter, so alone and aloof. And, despite drugs, her last days were bound to be difficult.

It was while praying for her and a long list of others that he got the idea. He wondered if there was a chance. It certainly couldn't hurt.

"Sara," he said tentatively, "I know you have a great deal on your mind, but I want to ask a favor. There's a family that needs extra support just now. Their four-year-old daughter is in a coma. She's in the last stages of leukemia. They need strength to get through this."

Sara seemed puzzled. "What has this got to do with me?"

"I need help. Sometimes it's just too much for me. I pray daily for the people of this hospital, but I could use another voice, another heart. I'm asking you to pray for the family of little Carrie, to ask God to put his loving arms around them."

"Chaplain, I don't mean to be rude, but it's been a long time since I prayed. With my diagnosis, if I had any inclination at all, it would be to pray for myself."

"You may certainly do that," he said. "But I'm asking you to pray for others." He took her hand. "Please, Sara, for me. I get so discouraged."

Before she pulled her hand away, she nodded briefly.

Two days later he came back. Little Carrie had slipped peacefully into the next world, and her parents were as honest in their grief and as strong as any he had ever seen in the loss of a child.

Now he asked another favor, for a teenager on a voluntary drug withdrawal program. The boy said he wanted to stay clean, but he feared he'd lose his nerve when he got back with his friends on the outside. Would she pray for him?

"I'm rusty," Sara said angrily. "Never did have the knack. I hated resorting to prayer only when I was in trouble, and it never occurred to me otherwise. It all seems so hypocritical."

"That's the reason I want you to pray for others," the chaplain said. "Surely you don't think God would question your motives in praying for Carrie's family or this teenager?"

She sighed. "It does give me something to do. When I begin to need a pain killer, I make myself pray for fifteen minutes before putting on the call light. It's silly, though."

On Tuesday he asked her to keep praying for the teenager, and also to add a man who'd suffered a stroke. The chaplain described the old fellow's frustration as he struggled to speak to his son and daughter-in-law. Though his hearing was not impaired, his family shouted their questions and encouragement. "They can't make out what he's trying to say," the chaplain said to Sara, "but instead of listening harder, they simply yell louder."

"How's the boy?" Sara moved carefully, onto her side. "The one fighting drugs? With all the drugs I'm taking for pain I can certainly identify with him."

"The doctors released him yesterday. I asked him to stop and see me when he comes in for his appointment with the psychologist. I told him there were at least two people here praying for him. Is the pain getting bad?"

She lifted an eyebrow. "I play a new game with myself now. As the shots get more frequent, I also increase the length of my prayers. When I can't stand it any longer, I give myself a reward. Morphine." She smiled. "A pay-off for praying."

The chaplain's heart leaped. Less than two weeks ago she had nothing to spare, no sympathy, no energy for anyone, not even herself. Now he shared the plights he'd just learned of: a middle-aged woman who needed a kidney transplant, and a young couple whose much wanted baby had been born with Down's syndrome.

The following week Sara's deterioration was obvious. She spoke hardly above a whisper, and the floor nurses said the end was near. The chaplain described successful laser treatment on the eyes of an artist with detached retinas.

The next day he told her about an older woman the doctors suspected of having bone cancer. Her condition turned out to be a fairly mild form of arthritis. The chaplain asked Sara to give thanks for these events and others taking place throughout the hospital and the city.

When the boy came to see the psychologist, the chaplain persuaded him to visit Sara. At her bedside he watched the street-wise youth grope for words. "I feel stronger now," the boy said, the wonder apparent in his voice. "It's gotta be coming from somewhere. I tried to kick it twice before, and it didn't work. I gotta believe you must have some influence, lady." He paused, struggling.

"The chaplain here, though, he told me you ain't doing so

good on your own case. I'm not in the know on this, but I been trying. I been…" He paused again. "I been pr-pr-praying for you." There. He'd said it. His glance went ceilingward, then back down at the woman in the bed. "Hang in there, lady." He hurried from the room.

Sara motioned the chaplain to come closer. He pulled a chair over so that their eyes were level. He recognized their pain, and also their joy.

"I saw through your little scheme almost from the start," she whispered. "But I still have to thank you. You've turned my last days into… into rather an interesting adventure."

"Don't thank me," the chaplain said, his voice husky. "Let's both thank him together." He took her dry hands in his and began firmly. "The Lord is my Shepherd, I shall not want…."

She joined him and they repeated the words slowly, softly, in unison. By the time they got to "surely goodness and mercy," he was saying the psalm alone. His silent thanks poured forth as he sat holding Sara's hands and watching her quiet, even breathing. For the first time in weeks, she slept without the help of drugs.

Carol V. Amen

He who bears another, is borne by another.
St. Gregory the Great

The Beautiful Teacup

A couple in England passed a china shop, which had a lovely teacup displayed in the window. They went inside to see it more closely, but suddenly the teacup spoke!

"You don't understand. I haven't always been a teacup. There was a time when I was a lump of red clay. My master took me and rolled me and patted me over and over. I screamed for him to stop, to leave me alone. But he continued to mold me, answering, 'Not yet.'

"Then I was placed on a wheel and spun around and around. It made me dizzy, spinning on and on like that. But he didn't stop when I was begging him to take me off the wheel. He continued shaping and molding, and then put me in an oven!

"I have never felt such intense heat! I wondered if he wanted me to burn up. And I screamed and beat on the door to get out. I could see the master through the opening. And I read his lips as he said, 'Not yet.'

"Finally, the door did open. He put me up on a shelf and I began to cool. That felt better. Then suddenly, he brushed me, and painted me all over. The fumes were terrible! I thought I would surely choke to death. I was gasping for air and hurting inside from the heat and choking fumes.

"Soon he put me into another oven. It wasn't the first one, but it was twice as hot! I knew for sure that this time I would suffocate. I begged my master to stop. All the time I could see him shaking his head and saying, 'Not yet.'

"I felt there was no help. I knew I could never make it. I was ready to give up. But just then the door opened. He took me out, and I could see that he was pleased with his work. He handed me a mirror and told me to look at myself. I did. And I said, 'That's not *me*. It couldn't be! I am so shiny and beautiful!'

"Then he said to me, 'I want you to know that I had to roll and pat you to shape you. If I had left you, then you would have dried up. And I know the wheel made you dizzy and sick, but if I had stopped, you would have crumbled. I know it hurt and was hot and disagreeable in the baking oven, but if I hadn't put you there, you would have cracked. I know the fumes were bad, when I brushed you and then painted you all over, but you see, if I hadn't done that, you would never have hardened. And if I hadn't put you in the second oven, you would not have survived for very long; you would have been brittle.'

"'Now you are a finished product. You are what I had in mind when I first began with you as a lump of clay!'"

Author Unknown

---

*People don't resist change as much as
the way they are changed.*
ANONYMOUS

Laughter Is a Gift

A thirty-eight-year-old scrubwoman would go to the movies and sigh. "If only I had her looks." She would listen to a singer and moan, "If only I had her voice."

Then one day someone gave her a copy of the book *The Magic of Believing.* She stopped comparing herself with actresses and singers. She stopped crying about what she didn't have and started concentrating on what she did have.

She took inventory of herself and remembered that in high school she had a reputation for being the funniest girl around. She began to turn her liabilities into assets. A few years ago Phyllis Diller made over one million dollars in a single year. She wasn't good-looking and she had a scratchy voice, but she could make people laugh.

Author Unknown

*How silent the woods would be
if only the best birds sang.*
ANONYMOUS

The Real Lessons

There was once a teacher whose "classroom" was a large city hospital where she visited sick children. One day she received a routine call from a certain child's regular teacher requesting that the hospital instructor visit her pupil. His class was studying nouns and adverbs, and with the right kind of assistance and help, it was hoped that the young lad would not fall behind in his homework.

Once the hospital teacher arrived at the boy's room, she realized that he was in the hospital's burn unit. No one had prepared her to find a young boy horribly burned over a good deal of his body and in great pain. She knew that she couldn't just turn and walk out, so she stammered for the right words, "I'm the hospital teacher, and your teacher sent me to visit with you and to help you with nouns and adverbs."

The hospital teacher was approached the next day by a nurse from the burn unit who asked her, "What did you do to that boy yesterday?" Before the teacher could finish offering a host of apologies, the nurse interrupted her: "You don't understand what I'm trying to say. We've been very worried about him. His spirits have been so low. He seemed to have lost all hope. But ever since you were here yesterday, his whole attitude is different. He's fighting back and finally responding to treatment. Once you left him it's as though he's decided to go on living." The hospital teacher thought over everything that she had said and done and nothing stood out in her mind that would have made such a radical change in the boy's behavior.

The boy later explained that he had completely given up all hope in life. But once he saw the hospital teacher he viewed things in a whole new way. It was a matter of coming to a simple conclusion. With tears in his eyes the boy was able simply to say: "I didn't think they would send a teacher to work on nouns and adverbs with a dying boy, would they?"

Author Unknown

The passion to get ahead is sometimes born of the fear lest we be left behind.
ERIC HOFFER

SEVEN

LOVE ADDS a LITTLE CHOCOLATE... TO WISDOM

*Speak kind words and
you will hear kind echoes.*

BAHN

174

Seeing Is Believing

Use your eyes today as if you would be stricken blind tomorrow. If I had three days to see, this is what I would want to see. On the first day I would want to see the people whose kindness and companionship have made my life worth living. I would call in my friends and look for a long time into their faces. I would also look into the face of a newborn baby. I would like to see the many books that have been read to me.

The next day I would get up early to see the dawn. I would visit a museum to learn of man's upward progress in the making of things. I would go to an art museum to probe the human souls by studying paintings and sculpture.

The third morning I would again greet the dawn, eager to discover new beauties in nature. I would spend this last day in the haunts of persons, where they work. I would stand at a busy street corner, trying to understand something of the daily lives of persons by looking into their faces and reading what is written there.

On the last evening I would go to a theater and see a hilariously funny play, so as to appreciate the overtones of humor in the human spirit. Yes, by God's light in Christ, seeing what matters and beholding the extraordinary in the commonplace.

Helen Keller

A Warm Place

Mynot, North Dakota, had incredible blizzards—I'm talking second-story blizzards where you could jump from the second story onto the snow. We were in the middle of one of those blizzards one day, and my father, who traveled a lot, was gone. My mother, who was a tiny but very determined person, had all three of us children home with the mumps. We were all alone in the house, with snow piled up all around the windows.

Perhaps she was a little nervous in this situation, but she created this wonderful, comfortable time. It was close to Christmas. And all three of us, our swollen heads tied up in handkerchiefs for the mumps, were gathered around her in the warm kitchen as she read Dickens' *A Christmas Carol*. It was wonderful.

From that experience I think I distilled the knowledge that even in the worst of situations you can create a warm place. You can even create your own reality.

Margaret Mason

. . . this time, like all times, is a very good one,
if we know what to do with it.
RALPH WALDO EMERSON

I'm Vulnerable...

And I want to take advantage of that vulnerability. I want to keep on being the new me.

Maybe I'll slide back with time. Perhaps my footprints in the sands of time won't be so crisp, so nicely edged, but instead will show that crumbling pattern of the one who slips back with each step almost as far as he strides. Maybe I'll go back to shaking hands instead of hugging. Maybe I'll fall back to choking off the tears instead of letting them flow. Maybe I'll want to be "strong" again instead of open.

I don't want to backslide. I don't want to fall off instead of weep out, but I know it can happen. When my chemotherapy is over, and the cards and the letters stop, and I have passed my five year test and can eat colored food again, what happens if I become the old, "strong" me again?

"Strong" isn't bad. It isn't everything, either.

I like the new me, who weeps to see the little neighbor girl ride her bright, pink bike, just because a healthy child in motion is such a beautiful sight.

I like the me who surprises men in gray suits with a big hug. It's a wonderful sight, two men in pinstripes, trying to figure out what to do with their briefcases while they attempt a hug—good laughter therapy if nothing else!

I like the me who talks to trees to let them know how well they are doing and how good they are looking.

I like the me who sings prayers, and laughs at silliness, and hopes all the time, without even knowing it, because it's so much a part of me.

I like the me who wakes up in the morning feeling joyful

that there is so much to do instead of burdened because there is so much to do.

I like the me who welcomes pain as a friend because it reminds me that I am alive.

I like the me who isn't bothered by the chaos of my desk but covers it over with the sure knowledge of what is important and what is not.

I like the me who trusts the Spirit more than the calendar and date books and lists and planners.

I've always had the cool, silent, determined courage of strength. Now I have the warm, bubbling, winging courage of weakness as well.

So I pray: "Let me grow, in both health and illness, into the new me. Let me be worthy of the new me. Let me be thankful for the old me—for the old me was a gift, too—but keep me vulnerable. Let every part of me move toward the whole me."

John Robert McFarland

Life is to live in such a way as not to be afraid to die.
St. Teresa of Avila

Pete's Place

I am generally not choosy about who works on my car. If a mechanic knows what to do about the whirring noises coming from my engine, who cares if he has dirt under his fingernails, or that his hair is shoulder length and looks like it hasn't been washed for two weeks?

At least that's how I thought I would feel. But today, riding cold on the heels of one of Chicago's most bitter winter chills, I was brought face to face with my preconceived notions about what is and what is not acceptable, even when it comes to the person who works on my car.

I was about three miles from home when a strange knocking sound began in my motor. This was not the day to be taking risks with my car. The thermometer outside the kitchen window read twenty below at 6 A.M. when I first ventured a look. I did not relish a walk in the frozen tundra. Fortunately, I was almost directly in front of our local gas station when the strange noises began.

Fine folks they are, these people at the gas station, I thought to myself. I had done small business with them before. The station is clean and litter free; the help are neatly uniformed with wide, white smiles, like the station attendants you once saw in the Texaco commercials on television. I had no second thoughts as I turned my Pontiac 6000 into their driveway, found an attendant, and explained my dilemma.

"Sorry, lady. We are booked for the next month and a half. With all this below-zero weather, it's been a zoo around here."

I thought perhaps he had misunderstood. I repeated my request, asking him to simply look under my hood and tell me whether my car was driveable. He refused. I tried again, thinking that perhaps an appeal to his emotions would work. "I can't take a chance in having to walk home in this kind of weather...."

He remained unbending. "Sorry, lady, there are twenty-five people with cars waiting before you. Everyone thinks their situation is an emergency."

I was left with one other option—leaving this garage and going to Pete's place. It used to be my kind of place. Pete had been our mechanic for years. Trusted. True. Dependable. And neat. Yes, neat. Every tool in its proper place. Not a trace of grease or dirt on his hands or uniform. And he even wore white shirts to work. Pete was a member of our church, and I liked his way of conducting business.

I had watched sadly when Pete sold his business and moved south. His once neat, well-kept garage looked more like a junkyard now that there were new owners. Today I knew I had no other choice. Pete's place was just around the corner.

I took a deep breath, and pushed open the door. A very large man with a stocking cap pulled down over his face sat leaning against the wall, apparently taking a nap. Dirty rags, piles of auto parts, tools, tires, and various strange shapes and sizes littered the room. A man with long blond hair and a dangling earring in one ear stood behind the counter, chewing on the end of a pencil.

I wanted to run from this place but the thought of walking home in sub-zero weather forced the words out of my mouth. "Could you please look under my hood and tell me about the knocking noise?"

The man with the dangling earring put down his pencil and sprang into action. "Be happy to, ma'am. Pull her right in here." And with that the large garage doors opened and I drove in among the canyon of junk.

The sleeping mechanic stirred, pulled his stocking cap from over his face, and lumbered over to a thermos of coffee. "Care for some coffee as you wait?" he asked with all the sincerity of a country gentleman.

An hour later, I'd forgotten the context. I'd been taken in by the care. The silver-earringed man had explained everything as he went along, and the man in the stocking cap served me coffee twice.

"It's not fixed permanently, Mrs. Senter. But it will get you home without blowing the engine. Now you just forget the pay. Glad I could help you." The mechanic slammed the hood, and as I left, I noticed the other man was back in his corner, asleep again.

Once safely home, I reflected on the junk-heap garage, the dangling-earringed mechanic, and the sleeping coffee-man. *I was a stranger and they took me in.* And what an interesting twist that I should be taken in by those I once considered "not my kind." Perhaps angels of mercy sometimes come dressed in different guise, so we can realize how blinding stereotypes can really be.

Ruth Senter

The Best Age

What is the best age of life to be alive?

This question was asked of a dozen people on a television program. One little girl said, "Two months, because you would be carried around. And you had lots of love and care."

Another child answered, "Three years, because you didn't have to go to school. You could do pretty much what you wanted, and could play most of the time."

A teenager said, "Eighteen. Because you are out of high school and you can drive a car wherever you want."

One girl said, "Sixteen, because you can have your ears pierced."

One man replied, "Age twenty-five. Because you have more pep." The man who answered was forty-three. He said he found it hard to walk up a hill now. He said at twenty-five he used to go till midnight, but now he is asleep by 9:00 P.M.

A three-year-old girl said the best age to be alive was twenty-nine. Because at that age you could lie around the house, sleep, and loaf most of the time. She was asked, "How old is your mother?" She replied, "Twenty-nine."

Someone thought forty was the best age because you are in the prime of life and vitality.

One lady answered fifty-five, because you are over your responsibilities of raising your children and can enjoy life and your grandchildren.

One man said sixty-five, because after that you can enjoy retirement.

The last person, an elderly woman said: "Every age is a good one. Enjoy the age you are now."

Author Unknown

Letting Go

To let go doesn't mean to stop caring; it means I can do it for someone else.

To let go is not to cut myself off, it's the realization that I can't control another.

To let go is not to enable, but to allow learning from natural consequences.

To let go is to admit powerlessness, which means the outcome is not in my hands.

To let go is not to try to change or blame another, I can only change myself.

To let go is not to care for, but to care about.

To let go is not to fix, but to be supportive.

To let go is not to judge, but to allow another to be a human being.

To let go is not to be in the middle arranging all the outcomes, but to allow others to affect their own outcomes.

To let go is not to be protective, it is to permit another to face reality.

To let go is not to deny but to accept.

To let go is not to nag, scold, or argue, but to search out my own shortcomings and to correct them.

To let go is not to adjust everything to my desires but to take each day as it comes and to cherish the moment.

To let go is not to criticize and regulate anyone but to try to become what I dream I can be.

To let go is not to regret the past but to grow and to live for the future.

To let go is to fear less and to love more.

Author Unknown

Assembling for Life

A man sent away for a new bicycle for his son at a very reasonable price. But when it arrived he was taken aback because he received a box full of parts that needed to be assembled. He carefully laid everything out, down to the last nut and bolt, on his garage floor. After reading and rereading the instructions many times, he still couldn't figure out how to put the bicycle together. He noticed his next door neighbor in his garage tinkering under the hood of his car. Since the neighbor was an old handyman, he decided to seek his assistance.

The man next door picked up the pieces that were scattered on the floor, studied each of them for a few minutes, and then began assembling the bicycle. In a relatively short amount of time he had it all put together.

"You're amazing!" said the man to his neighbor. "And you did it all without even looking at the instructions!"

"Few people know it," said the neighbor, "but I can't read, and when a person can't read, he's got to think."

Author Unknown

*Nearly everybody thinks less than he knows
and more than he thinks.*
ANONYMOUS

You Are As Young As...

Y outh is not a time of life, it is a state of mind.
Nobody grows old by merely living a number of years;
people grow old only by deserting their ideals.
Years wrinkle the skin, but to give up enthusiasm wrinkles
the soul. Worry, doubt, self-distrust, fear and despair—
these are the long, long years that bow the head and turn
the growing spirit back to dust.
Whether seventy or sixteen, there is in every being's
heart the love of wonder, the sweet amazement at the stars
and the starlike things and thoughts, the undaunted
challenge of events, the unfailing
childlike appetite for what next,
and the joy of the game of life.
You are as young as your faith, as old as your doubt;
as young as your self-confidence, as old as your fear;
as young as your hope, as old as your despair.

Author Unknown

Growth is the only evidence of life.
JOHN HENRY NEWMAN

Our Treasure

One night at dinner a husband and a wife were discussing a number of their affluent friends: their lavish homes, their expensive cars, and their wonderful vacations. Seeming a bit disheartened about their own financial plight, the wife remarked to her husband, "Someday we'll be rich."

He reached out, took her hand and replied, "Honey, we are rich. Someday we'll have money."

Author Unknown

What we obtain too cheaply we esteem too lightly;
it is dearness only that gives everything its value.
THOMAS PAINE

Bad or Good?

There is an ancient Chinese tale about a man who raised horses for a living. When one of his prized stallions ran off and could not be located, his friends gathered at his home to mourn his great loss. After they had expressed their concern, the man turned to them and asked: "How do I know whether what happened is bad or good?"

A few days went by and the runaway horse returned with several stray horses of considerable value following close behind him. The same acquaintances again came to his house, this time to celebrate his good fortune. "But how do I know whether it's good or bad?" the man asked them.

Later that day the horse kicked the owner's son and broke the young man's leg, severely injuring him. Once again the crowd gathered, this time to express their condolences for the accident. "But how do I know if this is bad or good?" the father asked once again.

A few days later, a terrible war broke out in their land. The man's son was exempted from military service because of his broken leg. Once again his friends gathered and...

Author Unknown

It is better to ask some questions than to know all of the answers.
JAMES THURBER

The Most Important Words

The six most important words:
"I admit that I was wrong."

The five most important words:
"You did a great job."

The four most important words:
"What do you think?"

The three most important words:
"Could you please..."

The two most important words:
"Thank you."

The most important word:
"We."

The least important word:
"I."

Author Unknown

Slowing Down

I might not go as quickly
As I did in years gone by,
But I plant my feet more firmly
And I choose my paths with care.

I might not see nor hear as well
As I did years ago,
But my feelings are much deeper
And I've lots more love to share.

I might be getting older,
But I've finally reached the stage
Where life's so very precious,
I just don't mind my age!

Alice Joyce Davidson

---

*It's no secret—the people who live long
are those who long to live.*
ANONYMOUS

The Winner

The loser is always part of the problem.

The winner is always part of the answer.

The loser always has an excuse.

The winner always has a program.

The loser says, "That is not my job."

The winner says, "Let me do it for you."

The loser sees a problem for every answer.

The winner sees an answer for every problem.

The loser sees a sand trap near every green.

The winner sees a green near every sand trap.

The loser says it may be possible but it is too difficult.

The winner says it may be difficult but it is possible.

Author Unknown

Go for the moon. If you don't get it,
you'll still be heading for a star.
WILLIS REED

EIGHT

LOVE ADDS *a* LITTLE CHOCOLATE... TO CHRISTMAS

*You cannot always have happiness,
but you can always give happiness.*
AUTHOR UNKNOWN

PEANUTS reprinted by permission of United Feature Syndicate, Inc.

The Unopened Gift

It was only because of his mother's pleading that the young man came home for Christmas. It was the last place he wanted to be because of a long-standing conflict he'd had with his father over a valuable piece of property. The young man wanted it then, and not as a part of his father's will.

The disagreement had started mildly enough, but it had grown through the years. It had become a wall between the father and his son. The father ached over it. He wanted things to be right between him and his son. If his son had only asked forgiveness, he would have deeded the property over to him immediately. The son just couldn't bring himself to that point.

The Christmas festivities were strained. When it came time to open presents, the son opened all of his except one—a tie-shaped box with a tag on it, "From Dad, with all my love." The son refused to open it, thinking it was one more tie.

After the family had gone to bed, the son sat staring at the box. He was haunted by the look on his dad's face when he had refused to open it. Suddenly he felt impelled to open the present.

As he unwrapped it, he realized it was not a tie as he had expected. Inside was the deed to the property. He rushed into his dad's bedroom and woke him up. Tears streamed down his face. "Dad, you made the first move. When I couldn't seem to change the way I was acting, you broke the bind! Forgive me... I love you."

Lloyd John Ogilvie

The Christmas Parade

One Christmas forty years ago shines in my memory as brightly as the Bethlehem star. But its beauty appeared only after family trauma.

My father had fallen at his construction job and broken his back. After surgery and a spinal fusion, he was confined to the house.

My mother took a waitressing job, and her wages barely paid the bills. Her tips bought our food and everything—or, more often, nothing—else. And thus evolved a family tradition: on counting nights, we'd dump all that week's change—her tips—onto the kitchen table. Because I was only five and the youngest, I counted the pennies. But I didn't mind; there were more of them than anything else. My seven-year-old sister counted nickels, our nine-year-old sister dimes, and Dad quarters. On the rare occasion we found a fifty-cent piece, we all sat and stared at it for awhile. Those were reserved to buy a family treat.

Based on the coins we had, Mom would then compile a grocery list. Sometimes we wondered how God would provide, but we never doubted Providence itself.

As the holiday season progressed, it turned out that counting time ended up falling the night before Christmas Eve this particular week. Naturally, we all hoped for a miracle. A miracle to buy food for Christmas dinner, to put presents under the sparse tree. But no miracle came.

My parents talked to us anxiously, begging our understanding, as we sat and prayed around the table. We didn't cry or argue or complain. Instead, we wrapped ourselves in hushed unity—it was an honesty that said, *We're all in this together, and we're going to be fine.*

The afternoon of Christmas Eve, Dad hobbled around the house while Mom worked. She was so late coming home that day, we had eaten without her, and she wasn't there to take my side on how awful the canned peas were, either. We three girls, who shared one upstairs room, dejectedly climbed into our beds. No money miracle, no reprieve for Christmas this year.

We awakened the next morning with no prospect of even a special supper. But after a simple family breakfast around the kitchen table, the unexpected came. From behind the backs of two grinning adults appeared three small, shining majorette batons! Then our parents presented white paper pleated skirts, tall white paper hats, and even cylinders of white paper to make our shoes look like boots.

We giggled! We jumped! We yelled! And then the parade began. Around the house, upstairs, downstairs, outside, around the block, we marched and counted and laughed our way right up to the meat loaf and leftovers, which tasted like a full-course Christmas dinner.

The light of the Christmas memory today, however, is the glow of our weary mother, who had talked the butcher out of a roll of his white paper. Our mother and incapacitated father cut and folded and stitched through the night to create three of the snazziest presents the world had ever seen, and had bought the three nineteen-cent majorette batons instead of part of that week's groceries. They couldn't buy presents, but refused to let that stop them from giving us gifts.

It's a shimmering, beautiful memory of how good it feels to grow up in a home where God has planted love.

Charlotte Forslund

Be it ever so humble, there's no place like home for wearing what you like.
GEORGE ADE

A Special Christmas Breakfast

~♥~

Until last year, the greatest sorrow of my life was that my wife, Alice, and I could not have any children. To make up for this in a small way, we always invited in all the children on our street to our house each Christmas morning for breakfast.

We would decorate the house with snowflakes and angels in the windows, a nativity scene, and a Christmas tree in the living room, and other ornaments that we hoped would appeal to the children. When our young guests arrived—there were usually ten or fifteen of them—we said grace and served them such delicacies as orange juice garnished with a candy cane (which could be used as a straw once it began to dissolve). And after the meal we gave each one of the youngsters a wrapped toy or game. We used to look forward to these breakfasts with the joyful impatience of children.

But last year, about six weeks before Christmas, Alice died. I could not concentrate at work. I could not force myself to cook anything but the simplest dishes. Sometimes I would sit for hours without moving, and then suddenly find myself crying for no apparent reason.

I decided not to invite the children over for the traditional Christmas breakfast. But I did not have to be alone for the holidays. Kathy and Peter Zack, my next-door neighbors, asked me to join them and their three children for dinner on Christmas Eve. As soon as I arrived and had my coat off, Kathy asked me, "Do you have any milk at your house?"

"Yes," I replied. "If you need some, I'll go right away."
"Oh, that's all right. Come and sit down. The kids have been

waiting for you. Just give Peter your keys and he can get it in a few minutes."

So I sat down, prepared for a nice chat with eight-year-old Beth and six-year-old Jimmy. (Their little sister was upstairs sleeping.) But my words wouldn't come. What if Beth and Jimmy should ask me about my Christmas breakfast? How could I explain to them? Would they think I was just selfish or self-pitying? I began to think they would. Worse, I began to think they would be right.

But neither of them mentioned the breakfast. At first I felt relieved, but then I started to wonder if they remembered it or cared about it. As they prattled on about their toys, their friends, and Christmas, I thought they would be reminded of our breakfast tradition, and yet they said nothing. This was strange, I thought, but the more we talked, they more I became convinced that they remembered the breakfast but didn't want to embarrass Grandpa Melowski (as they called me) by bringing it up.

I didn't have long to ponder this. Dinner was soon ready and afterward we all went to late mass. After mass, the Zacks let me out of their car in front of my house. I thanked them and wished them all Merry Christmas as I walked toward my front door. Only then did I notice that Peter had left a light on when he borrowed the milk—and that someone had decorated my windows with snowflakes and angels!

When I opened the door, I saw that the whole house had been transformed with a Christmas tree, a nativity scene, candles, and all the other decorations of the season. On the dining room table was Alice's green Christmas tablecloth and her pine-cone centerpiece. What a kind gesture! At that moment, I wished that I could still put on the breakfast, but I had made no preparations.

The next morning at about eight, a five-year-old with a package of sweet rolls rang my bell. Before I could ask him what was going on, he was joined by two of his friends, one with a pound of bacon, the other with a pitcher of orange juice. Within fifteen minutes, my house was alive with all the children on my street, and I had all the food I needed for the usual festive breakfast. I was tremendously pleased, although in the back of my mind I still feared that I would disappoint my guests. I knew my spur-of-the-moment party was missing one important ingredient.

At about nine-thirty, though, I had another surprise. Kathy Zack came to my back door.

"How's the breakfast?" she asked.

"I'm having the time of my life," I answered.

"I brought something for you," she said, setting a shopping bag on the counter.

"More food?"

"No," she said. "Take a look."

Inside the bag were individually wrapped packages, each bearing the name of one of the children in the dining room and signed, "Merry Christmas from Grandpa Melowski."

My happiness was complete. It was more than just knowing that the children would receive their customary gifts and wouldn't be disappointed; it was the feeling that everyone cared.

I like to think it's significant that I received a gift of love on the same day that the world received a sign of God's love two thousand years ago in Bethlehem. I never found out whom to thank for my Christmas present. I said my "Thank you" in my prayers that night—and that spoke of my gratitude more than anything I could ever say to my neighbors.

Harold Melowski

Only a life that is lived for others
is a life worthwhile.
ALBERT EINSTEIN

Christmas Dinner

One Christmas Eve, a prosperous businessman was hurrying to a butcher shop before closing time. "Buying your Christmas turkey?" a friend asked. "No. Hot dogs," he answered.

He then explained how, years before, a total business failure had suddenly wiped out his fortune. He had faced Christmas with no job, no money for gifts and less than a dollar for food. That year he and his wife and small daughter said grace before dinner and ate hot dogs—"a whole kennel of them," he laughed. His wife had given each frankfurter toothpicks for legs and broom straws for tails and whiskers. Their daughter had been enchanted, and her infectious delight spread merriment among them all. After dinner they gave thanks again for the most loving and festive time they'd ever had.

"Now it's a tradition," the man said. "Hot dogs for Christmas—to remind us of that happy day when we realized we still had one another and our ability to laugh and celebrate."

Author Unknown

The crisis of yesterday is the joke of tomorrow.
H.G. WELLS

The Spirit of Christmas Giving

Several years ago a thirteen-year-old boy who attended Mohawk Central School in Paines Hollow, New York, heard an appeal for contributions to Santa Claus Anonymous, a group that provides gifts for unfortunate children that otherwise would go without Christmas presents.

The boy struggled to save a few pennies for this purpose. On the Friday before Christmas vacation he had fifteen cents and planned to turn in this small treasure at the school that day. But a furious blizzard blasted the area that Friday and the school buses could not run.

So the boy waded a considerable distance through the deep snow to give his fifteen cents to the school principal. The principal found it difficult to control his emotions as he accepted the gift, for the youngster was one of the destitute children listed to receive a Christmas present from Santa Claus Anonymous.

Author Unknown

Charity, to be fruitful, must cost us.
MOTHER TERESA

The Landlady's Christmas Gift

Forging ahead through driving November rains, I hurried to my home in Vancouver, British Columbia. Home was a basement suite I rented in a large old house. When I flicked on the lights, I noticed something peculiar on my small kitchen table. A cooking pot had been turned upside down, revealing blistered handles. "Will you be more careful?" said a note. "Turn down the gas when food begins to boil." It was signed by Lily, the landlady.

Tears sprang to my eyes. All afternoon, I'd jostled crowds in noisy shopping malls, seeking a perfect Christmas gift for my mother, but every time I'd come upon something I knew she'd like, it was too expensive for me. Saving money for nursing school and living expenses didn't leave me much for Christmas gifts. Totally discouraged, I'd taken the bus home. It seemed unfriendly to me to sit shoulder to shoulder with people without saying a word, so I'd started a conversation with the woman beside me. She'd answered me curtly, then stared out the window as though wanting to be left alone. Then I came home to find this rebuke from my landlady.

A country girl living on her own in the big city of Vancouver—the idea seemed so glamorous a few months ago. Now, crushing loneliness overwhelmed me. I threw myself across my bed behind a curtain and sobbed out my heart.

Eventually, I lay there thinking and praying about a suitable gift for my mother. Suddenly I remembered a conversation I'd overheard at work. Some women had discussed a home party they'd attended. A saleswoman had come to demonstrate her wares and, because sales had reached a certain amount, the hostess received a lace tablecloth for her efforts. "There were only about ten people there," the woman had said, "but it's surprising how fast sales mount up when everybody buys a little."

A lace tablecloth! What could be more perfect for my mother for Christmas? I could just see her worn hands smooth it across the table in our old farmhouse kitchen. On Christmas day, as on other special occasions, she'd place roast chicken, still hot in its juices, on that small table (we couldn't afford turkey), mashed potatoes whipped with an egg until they glistened, spicy crab apples, feather-light buns, German Pfeffernuesse and Lebkuchen....

The more I thought about that lace tablecloth, the more I wanted it. But a home party? Could I really carry that off? I'd never done anything like that before. Besides, who would come to it?

Well, there were people at church. I didn't know anybody there really well, but they might come. And then there were the women I'd had lunch with at work. I counted them up: yes, there were at least ten.

"Oh, Lord, if this is your will, give me the courage to do it," I prayed.

Still full of self-doubt, I booked a party. Encouraged by the saleswoman's enthusiastic response, I distributed my carefully written invitations at church and at work.

The day of the party in early December dawned heavy and gray. I decorated my scrubbed basement suite with cedar boughs and placed a red candle and Christmas napkins beside the dishes I'd borrowed from the landlady. By evening my place smelled of cedar, chocolate brownies, and coffee.

Half an hour before the party was to start, the saleswoman arrived with a load of boxes. I helped her carry them inside, and soon a lovely display of colorful kitchenware and toys decorated my bed, the only flat area big enough.

I offered the woman a cup of coffee. Cradling my own mug in clammy hands, I glanced at the clock again with one ear cocked to outside noises. Where were my guests? Only five minutes to go and nobody had come yet.

Promptly at 7:30 P.M. the door burst open; it was Lily, my landlady. Her eyes swept the empty room, and she blurted out, "Where is everybody?"

"I don't know, Lily," I stammered. "Nobody has come yet."

"Well, we can't wait much longer," she said and stomped out of the room.

I groaned inwardly, thinking that I should have known better than to book a party.

"I suppose we'll call it off," the saleswoman said, as she rose and began to gather up her wares.

Apologizing for the inconvenience I'd caused her, I helped her pack. Toys swam before my eyes. Embarrassment burned my cheeks.

Suddenly, I heard a noise outside and the door opened, framing two women I'd never seen before. "Hi! We live down the street. Lily tells us there's a party here."

Bewildered, I asked them to take a seat.

During the next ten minutes this scenario repeated itself several times. The room filled with people. I stared incredulously at each unfamiliar, yet friendly face. Finally Lily herself returned, wearing a grin, and winked at me.

Over coffee, the buzzing of animated voices reminded me of other gatherings of friendly people at home in the country.

"Going home for Christmas?" somebody asked me.

When I shook my head no, Lily quickly intercepted: "I'd like you to have turkey dinner with us. And by the way, next week we're having a Christmas cantata at church. Are you interested?" Other invitations followed for coffee and Christmas baking.

I could hardly grasp the good will of these people who an hour ago had been total strangers to me. Perhaps people seem unfriendly because they've lacked opportunity to prove otherwise, I mused.

Oh, you're wondering about the lace tablecloth? When the sales were totaled I had enough for the coveted hostess gift. For many years my mother decked her old table with it, and her face revealed the pride and gratitude she felt.

But Lily herself gave the greatest gift that Christmas: underneath her brusque manner lay a warm, caring heart that reached out to ease my loneliness. Lily gave me a gift for my mother and a home for Christmas.

Helen Grace Lescheid

A Christmas Special

~♥~

During the Depression, many families could scarcely afford the bare essentials, much less purchase presents at Christmas. "But, I'll tell you what we can do," said the father to his six-year-old son, Pete. "We can use our imaginations and make pictures of the presents we would like to give each other."

For the next few days, each member of the family worked secretly, but with joy. On Christmas morning, huddled around a scraggly tree decorated with pitifully few decorations, the family gathered to exchange the presents they had created. And what gifts they were!

Daddy got a shiny black limousine and a red motor boat. Mom received a diamond bracelet and a new hat. Little Pete had fun opening his gifts, a drawing of a swimming pool and pictures of toys cut from magazines.

Then it was Pete's turn to give his present to his parents. With great delight, he handed them a brightly colored crayon drawing of three people—a man, woman, and little boy. They had their arms around one another and under the picture was one word: US. Even though other Christmases were far more prosperous for this family, no Christmas in the family's memory stands out as more precious!

Author Unknown

A Homecoming

It was a simple question my seven-year-old daughter asked me about six weeks before Christmas: "What can we get Grandpa for a gift this year?"

Grandpa, who would be ninety on his next birthday, lived in a mobile home on our extra lot, practically next to our kitchen windows. We had moved both grandparents two years before when Grandma became an invalid and they both needed more daily care. The previous Christmas had been a rather dismal one, with Grandma so sick. She died just two weeks later.

For some fifteen years now, Grandpa's youngest daughter, Jeanne, had been in a state institution. I knew that it had been at least four or five years since Grandpa had last seen her. Due to Grandma's illness, my own husband's two-year battle to overcome mental illness, and our son's serious asthma condition, we had not been able to bring her home for her yearly week's vacation. Our three youngest children, ages seven, nine, and eleven, could barely remember her.

I explained the situation to them, then asked what they thought about my plan to bring Jeanne home for a week during the holidays, letting them know that this would be a gift to Grandpa and Daddy from us. I found they were more than willing to help in any way they could. The following day I wrote for the required vacation forms from the hospital, and also asked if it would be possible for her to travel by bus.

A few days later the reply came, assuring us that she could handle the bus trip. Jeanne was a gentle, quiet patient. It was only her mind that had never developed beyond that of a five- or six-year-old.

Now the real spirit of the season came into the picture. The children decided to forego their usual gift exchange, using the money to buy the bus ticket and a few needed articles for Jeanne's gifts. Jeanne would arrive on the evening of December 23. Although it would have been fun to surprise Grandpa, I was fearful it might be too much for him, so we told him a few hours before the bus arrived.

I will never forget the look of pride and happiness on my children's faces when Grandpa thanked them. "I thought I would never see Jeanne again," he said, "and now she will be right here for Christmas!" As he spoke, the tears flowed freely down his wrinkled cheeks, and I realized what must have been in his heart many times during the past years.

Jeanne was like any youngster, with a dozen things to tell about her bus ride. When we arrived home from the bus station, Jeanne went straight to Grandpa and said, "Oh, Papa! I'm so glad to see you! And there's my brother too! How are you anyhow?" There was not a dry eye in the room.

The next two days were busy ones. Jeanne followed me everywhere, her eyes filled with excitement like my own children's. We took her and Grandpa to church for Christmas. Jeanne knelt quietly, her hands folded. She remembered how to pray!

While the school children sang the stirring, familiar carols, my husband and I knew within our hearts that this truly was a Christmas filled with meaning for us. And our children had learned compassion for someone not blessed with the ability to learn and do things we often take for granted.

Rita Blanchette

A Walk for Love

A boy living on a remote island in Hawaii listened intently as his teacher explained why people gave presents on Christmas Day. "The gift is an expression of our love and our joy over the birth of Jesus, who is the greatest gift of all," she said.

When Christmas Day arrived, the boy brought the teacher a gift—a sea shell with a sparkling beauty that was rarely seen on anything that washed up from the ocean. "Where did you ever find such a unique and marvelous shell?" the teacher asked.

The young boy told her that there was only one place he knew of where such extraordinary shells were to be found. There was a certain bay over twenty miles away that was very hidden and secluded where these shells washed ashore on occasion.

"Why...why, it's absolutely gorgeous. I will treasure it for a lifetime," said the teacher. "But you shouldn't have gone all that way to get a gift for me."

Remembering her lesson on gift-giving, the boy's eyes brightened and he said, "Long walk part of gift."

Author Unknown

It is only the souls that do not love
that go empty in this world.
ROBERT HUGH BENSON

ACKNOWLEDGMENTS

Love Adds a Little Chocolate from *Illustrations Unlimited* edited by James S. Hewett. © 1988. Reprinted by permission of Tyndale House Publishers, Inc. All rights reserved.

Encounter in a Boutique. Reprinted by permission of Gloria J. Gibson. © 1991 Gloria J. Gibson.

Bootless Tears. Reprinted by permission of Sr. Mary Corita Sweeney, R.S.M. © 1993 Sr. Mary Corita Sweeney, R.S.M.

All the Time in the World. Reprinted from *God's Little Devotional Book for Dads* with permission of Honor Books (Tulsa: Honor Books, © 1995).

Sacrifice. Reprinted by permission of Leslie B. Flynn. From *Come Alive with Illustrations* © 1987 Leslie B. Flynn.

New Life for an Old Skirt by Amy Holloway. Reprinted from *The Common Ground Book: A Circle of Friends* by Remar Sutton and Mary Abbot Waite. © 1992. Reprinted by permission.

Surprise! Reprinted from *God's Little Devotional Book for Dads* with permission of Honor Books (Tulsa: Honor Books, © 1995).

The Friendly Fisherman. Reprinted by permission of Katherine Karras. © 1992 Katherine Karras.

Good News. Reprinted by permission of Medard Laz. © 1997 Medard Laz.

When God Says "No" by Medard Laz. Reprinted by permission of Medard Laz. © 1997.

Loving You from *Bus 9 to Paradise* by Leo F. Buscaglia, Ph.D. Published by Slack, Inc. Reprinted by permission of Leo F. Buscaglia, Inc. © 1986.

ABOUT THE AUTHOR

Medard Laz (or Med, as he is often called) is well-known for his entrepreneurial abilities. Med was instrumental in the spread of *Marriage Encounter* from its earliest days. These weekends that help couples to take a good marriage and make it better have spread throughout the world. Over two million couples have been enriched as a result.

Med also helped to foster the growth of *The Beginning Experience* throughout the world, serving on its national board, helping set up teams around the country, and representing *The Beginning Experience* on *The Phil Donahue Show*. *The Beginning Experience* provides a weekend experience where those who have lost a spouse through divorce or death work through their grief and their anger and are able to begin a new life.

With Suzy Yehl Marta, Med Laz co-founded *Rainbows for All God's Children*. *Rainbows* is a support group for children and teens who have experienced divorce or death in their family. With trained adult guidance and support, over 600,000 young people in over sixteen countries have been helped in their journey to a new life.

With Charlotte Hrubes, Med founded *Joyful Again!*—a support weekend for widowers and widows, enabling them to work through their grief, anger, and guilt after the death of a loved one.

Med Laz is the author of nine books, among them *The Six Levels of a Happy Marriage, Helps for the Separated and Divorced, Helps for the Widowed, After a Loved One Dies*, and *Making Parish Meetings Work*.

Med is a highly sought-after speaker, giving presentations

and workshops on a variety of marriage and family issues as well as topics related to spiritual growth.

Med Laz lives in Chicago and is a priest of the Archdiocese of Chicago, having founded Holy Family Parish Community in Inverness, Illinois. You can contact him to schedule speaking engagements or author appearances by mail at:

Med Laz
c/o Servant Publications
P.O. Box 8617
Ann Arbor, MI 48107

You can be a contributor to a future volume of *Love Adds a Little More Chocolate*. If you have a story or a poem similar to what you have read, please send it to the above address. Enclose a S.A.S.E. (self-addressed stamped envelope). Each submission should be no longer than 1,000 words. Please send typed, double-spaced manuscripts. Be sure to provide the source.